AF431001

WHERE BLACK RULES WHITE

Where Black Rules White

A JOURNEY ACROSS AND ABOUT HAYTI

Hesketh-Prichard

Abdul Alhazred

Forbidden Books

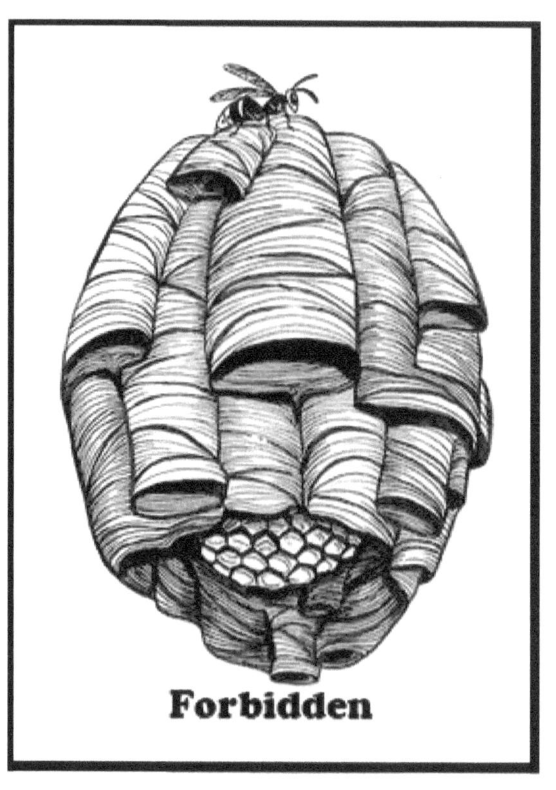

ISBN: 9798869388469
E-Book ISBN: 9798869390196
This edition was formatted and prepared for Forbidden Books
by Abdul Alhazred.

Forward

There is no right to the status of barbarism.
-John Burgess,
Foundations of Political Science

Haiti has the distinction of being the only republic founded by a slave revolt and the second republic founded in the Western hemisphere in 1804. After a dramatic slaughter of the white and mixed population of the island, during which a minority of the European and mullatto population succeeded in fleeing, the hermit republic was isolated by the Western world. An initial euphoria of plunder settled into an impoverished indolence until the Haitian government paid a famous indemnity of 100 million francs in exchange for the diplomatic recognition of France and the trade and capital desperately needed from the outside world. Thus, the hermit republic became accessible, yet fiercely guarded its own interests as she understood them: famously building colossal fortifications with forced labor and investing scarce resources into a military with more officers than infantry. Nevertheless, Haiti managed to conquer the entire island of Hispaniola in 1822, banning men of European ancestry from owning land, expropriating church lands, and subjugating the Spanish speaking population of the eastern half of the island. The Dominicans launched a successful war of independence against the Haitians in 1844 and divided the island.

Attempting to restore its former military glories, resources were diverted to modern weapons in the 1850's and 60's. After US recognition in 1862, the Haitian navy purchased the leaky and experimental Confederate ironclad, the CSS Atlanta, which had to be constantly bailed to save her from sinking in the sheltered wharf of Savannah. Under tow on the east coast, the baffling investment disappeared *en route* to Haiti and apparently sank with all hands an 1869. The same year, President U. S. Grant, frustrated with Reconstruction and seemingly careless about the recent recognition of Haiti, contemplated the annexation of the new Dominican Republic and the colonization of the island with the Freedmen of the Reconstruction South. Grant's treaty failed only with a tied vote in the Senate.

The political adventures of the hapless republic are obscure and farcical. Presidents, military dictators, self-declared kings and even emperors sometimes succeeded in making deals with foreign capital, more often provoked foreign intervention, and sometimes managed to build monuments that outlasted the grandiose titles and ambitions they always proclaimed. Consistently, the Haitian leadership has proclaimed its legitimacy based in the liberation of its masses from slavery and the self-determination of its people: concepts familiar enough to the enlightened West, but enigmatic for the true believers of liberalism. Although self-determined, Haitians were perpetually victimized by predatory rulers: their "elective kings" and cannibal priests. The rhetoric of Western enlightenment met the lowest standard of living in the Western world in Haiti. The execution of a former president was followed by the lynching of the sitting president in early 1915, and a revolutionary environment preceded the occupation of the Republic by the United States Marines. The force left a semblance of government in place while they collected the taxes and ran the treasury. The Marines would occupy Haiti for almost twenty years. Thus began the long and bizarre relationship between the befuddled Americans and the Voodoo Caribbean. Somehow, the Americans never lost confidence that circumstances in Haiti could be rectified for progress in Haiti, for the Americans believe, above all, in the "self-evident" truth that "all men are created equal." Any differences between a Bostonian and a Haitian are obviously unimportant.

Today, the circumstances of Haiti are almost unbelievably bad. According to the World Bank, Haiti has a GDP per capita of $1,694, which is half of the second most-hopelessly poor American country, Honduras. Haiti has the lowest life-expectancy in the Western Hemisphere, at 63.1, which is, at least, higher than that of Liberia and Afghanistan. Haiti's GDP is higher than that of Jamaica, at $38.9 billion, but this is overwhelmingly due to foreign aid from Europe and the Anglosphere, which continue to tell themselves fanciful stories about guilt and responsibility for former slaves, although self-determined from the bloody year of 1804. The GDP has dropped by 3.3% in 2020, 1.8% in 2021, and 1.68% in 2022, and 1.9% in 2023, according to the World Bank. Irresponsible methods of deforestation without any cultural effort to renew the natural resources has resulted in the near total destruction of the forests of the country, the erosion of the topsoil, and finally the widespread desertification of the country as the ground transforms into sterile hardpan. In 2022, the trade imbalance was a terrifying $1.35 billion in exports with $5.45 billion in imports! The CIA World

Factbook estimates that over 20% of the economy in the 2020's is made up of remittances from the Haitian diaspora.

The last President of Haiti, Jovenel Moïse, as assassinated in his home in 2021, allegedly by a narcotics gang. Three years later, somehow still without a presidential election, Prime Minister Ariel Henry fled Port-au-Prince as government forces retreated in the face of the warlord and alleged voodoo cannibal known as "Barbeque." The realities of Haiti belie the official pronouncements of an interim government following the resignation of the impotent Henry in the summer of 2024. The country is ruled by gangs who battle the police and army in the streets. The port of the capital and the airport remain closed as armed gangs seize the productive farms, and the World Food Programme warns of five million of Haiti's eleven million population "face crisis or acute levels" of hunger. Anxious to keep European "peacekeepers" out of Haiti, the UN was considering a garrison of Kenyan troops in Haiti before the government collapsed and fled in early 2024. Once again, foreign intervention seems inevitable to restore a modicum of order to prevent mass starvation.

What is a Constitution? Is it not merely the solution to the following problem? Given the population, the mores, the religion, the geographic situation, the political circumstances, the wealth, the good and bad qualities of a particular nation, to find the laws that suit it.
-Joseph De Maistre

Haiti suffers from the assumptions and core beliefs of Westerners, who have intervened and influenced the destiny of the nation in countless ways. Today, as in 1804, the people of Haiti suffer inside the limits of Western political tolerances created in the Enlightenment. Like the Americans, the Haitians embraced a revolutionary idea of equality and revolted against their imperial order to establish a republic. Like the Americans, the Haitians fell back on their own traditions and resources with an isolation policy, and only later developed strong relationships with outside powers. Like Americans, Haitians took the law, language, and religion of their mother country and this continues to influence their character and destiny today. Unlike Americans, Haitians did not share the same blood.

The liberal ideology is built on the abstract assertion, divorced from all experience, that man is made exclusively from his environment, and so Westerners have assumed on these grounds that all nations can homogenize and become equal under a liberal order. Locke's assumption of the "blank slate" and Rousseau's assumption that all inequalities are artificial undergird a uniquely Western idealism unsupported by our most basic experiences of the realities of human differences. Any consideration of history reveals two categories of differences that divide and unite mankind.

Haitians acquired French from their former empire, but commonly speak their famous patois. Haitians were gifted the Catholic Church by their empire, but have popularly preferred their African voodoo. The Haitians formally use the Code Napoleon, but informally follow personal loyalties to gangs and factions who periodically massacre each other. While the Americans inherited church, law, and mores from the English while sharing the blood ancestry, the key difference in Haiti was the lack of blood inheritance and the violent severance of ties to their only source of Western civilization: the white and mixed French colonists massacred in the Haitian revolution. Thus, it has always been unreasonable to expect Haiti to fit into a Western mold.

Politics is the art of the possible, as Bismarck said. All history is conflict between better and worse visions of order. In Haiti, the liberal order imposed from the outside by the West has been ab abject failure. Any number impositions of order are kept out of discussion for fear of the bugbear of "authoritarianism" and the curtailment of "liberties" that have made the "republic" a living hell. Anyone with a mind to have mercy on the failed state of Haiti will impose strict order through the military, declare the benighted Haitians incapable of governing themselves, and bring the hammer down on the cannibal priests and drug lords who terrorize the population.

No Western country is now capable of taking on the stern responsibility of empire, and if they were capable, why do it? France and the US have the best reasons to act. France, because it is her own bastard, patricide, self-immolating offspring. The US because of the consequences of millions of starving voodoo practitioners adding to the chaos of her own border and demographics. In the end, self-interest will mean at least a blockade of the horror that is Haiti, but will more likely mean the invitation of her desperate hoards to resettle elsewhere. Ironically, this approach reassures the liberals and finds some success, but only because civilization is imposed and better social norms predominate practically everywhere but Haiti.

Man is made of his inherited nature and his experiences. He is not entirely one or the other, and is capable of rising above and falling below both. Haiti's national isolation has emphasized a failure of liberalism to appreciate both aspects of human nature and this has resulted in the unnecessary cruelty that is the history of the independent Haiti.

Abdul Alhazred
Sanaá
Summer of 2024

Contents

1

First Impressions of the Black Republic

The liner was hove to, awaiting daylight. Across the leaden swell Hayti lay hazy and of a soft grey, her delicate mountain crests cut sharply out against the brightening sky. Soon the east was alive and glowing in deep orange and deeper red patched with livid green, a bar of angry colour shut in between the sea and a jagged lid of cloud. Four bells rang forward, and upon the stroke we were under way and steaming slowly past the dim dead shores. Between us and the distant heights ran a low bluff, bristling with scrub.

No villages were visible, but here and there, through glasses, we could discern a brownish speck which might have been a solitary hut, but these did not break the sense of desolation. Nothing seemed alive save the dawn and a clean, sweet wind that blew graciously cool after the sweltering heats of the night.

Thus it was that in November of last year (1899) I saw Hayti for the second time. Eighteen months had elapsed since I first steamed along under the same shores, and Hayti had lost none of her mystery and fascination. Since the wholesale massacre of the whites by order of General Dessalines, which followed immediately upon the proclamation of the Act of Independence in 1804, Hayti has been a sealed land. Very little could be told about her; for very little was known. Threaded in the circle of a hundred civilised isles, she alone has drawn a veil between herself and the rest of mankind.

A few scores of white men live in her coast towns, but of the interior even they can tell you practically nothing. The Black Republic, set between her tropical seas and virgin mountain-peaks, keeps her secrets well.

In spite of endless inquiries, until I actually landed in the island, I could gather no definite details. The ship I was travelling in passed seven times a year along the southern coast to drop the mails at the principal port of Jacmel, but although many people on board had lived half their lives on the neighbouring islands, I could glean no information respecting Hayti. I was vaguely told that the place was unhealthy, more unhealthy than Colon, and even more abnormally dirty, and that men were rather more apt to die suddenly there than elsewhere in the tropics. Even the steamer seemed to hold herself aloof. It is her custom to lie well out in the roadstead of Jacmel, and she only waits for the return of the mail boat before putting to sea again.

BANANAR AT JACMEL.

There were of course various strange rumours drifting about, stories that had oozed out from the guarded silence shrouding those dark-green shores, stories of snake-worship, and poisonings, human sacrifice and cannibalism. Hayti appeared to be a stage with the curtain down, — all the world knew that the dramas of life and death were being played out over and over again behind that curtain, but with what curious or horrible variations from the ordinary tenor of human existence none could guess. I had read one or two books about the place, notably that by Sir Spencer St. John, who was British Minister in Hayti for a considerable period, but even his book was some years old.

Hayti the Mysterious! Her appeal to the imagination is inevitable. Ships from Europe and America move perpetually round and along her coasts and call at her open ports, ocean cables link her to the rest of the globe, but for all these things, five miles inland you lose touch with civilisation, with the world.

From the sea, her mountains, bearded with dark forests up to their wrinkled brows, scowl at you. To deny that she is picturesque is impossible ; to do so would be to acknowledge a sheer lack of imagination.

Mile after mile we slid along the coast cliff, until the fjord-like bay turned in upon itself, and there was the town of Jacmel lying inside its belt of sand.

Jacmel from the sea is not unlike towns in the Colombian Republic or on the Pacific coast. The same white houses, nestling in vivid foliage, give it the same false air of coolness.

Five minutes later the quarter-boat was shouldering her way shorewards across the swell which broke in foam almost at the foot of the palms.

We shot past the reefs, and I scrambled on to the dilapidated landing-stage among the crowd of negroes, — a crowd which as to colour represented every shade of full-bodied black. As to dress, there were degrees from gold lace down to the simplicity of a cloth with a hole in the middle for the wearer's head, supplemented by ragged trousers. Most of them carried heavy jointed clubs. The boat that had landed me put oft'; I saw the rowers slide into their stroke ; I waited till they reached the shadow of the steamer, the gangway was raised, the boat swung inboard, and the liner dived away over the glinting sea. Then I turned, stepped from the boarding, and was on Haytian earth.

I do not know precisely what I had expected, but I do know that it was not at all like the reality.

Almost straight before me was a narrow street, lined with irregular buildings, something like a street of old London as you see it in pictures, save that the overhanging first floors were wooden piazzas.

I walked slowly along, taking the measure of things. It was a dirty street, albeit the chief one of the chief town of southern Hayti, and the sun was scalding. The place was also a crush with human beings of African race and their donkeys. A lean dog or two basked in the alleys. There were shops, open cavernous places, with the stock-in-trade of the proprietor depending from ropes round the walls. Pavement or foot-path there was none.

The piazzas, jutting from the upper floors of the ungainly houses, were supported by pillars of wood driven into the earth; but walking under them in the shadow was an athletic exercise of four-foot leaps up and down, for some of the domiciles possessed brick thresholds leading to the supports, while others had none. There were many empty houses with smashed shutters, fire-scarred shells which seemed all the emptier for the pitiless sunlight. In Hayti they always start a revolution by firing the town.

I turned on the thought to observe the negroes in their own preserve, where they may " revolute " as they like. Most of them had dropped their work or business to look at me. Through the dust and glare wizened donkeys trotted, laden with huge bundles of guinea-grass, negresses hawked about baskets of bananas and mangoes, the street was full of men and women, screaming, gesticulating, and shouting. A bareheaded negro was blowing a tin trumpet in long, ringing blasts. The din was incredible.

There were women carrying loads upon their heads ; one was half-running with a bottle balanced on a yellow bandana tied round her brows. Most of them were dressed in white, short-kilted to the knee, and nearly all wore the turban handkerchief. As for the men, some had coats, some only trousers, and some, more ragged than

the rest, affected kepis with red bands. These last I discovered later
were policemen.

No carriages were to be seen, not even a broken-down West
Indian buggy. It was my first impression of the land where Black
rules White. The bawl and clatter of voices, the jostling crowd, the
scream of an angry man in the hot street, the few cool stores with
their proprietors seated on chairs in the doorways, the ungainly
wooden houses with their sprawling side-posts, the sun, the smell,
the dirt : — this was Hayti.

The British Consular Agent, to whom I had brought a letter
of introduction, was most kind, and offered to put me up for the
night, a proposal which I was only too glad to accept. Failing this
hospitaHty I should have been obliged to bivouac in the open; for
Jacmel, though the principal port in southern Hayti, does not boast
either hotel or resthouse where one could hope for a night's shelter.

Half an hour later, as I sat at peace in the Consular office, near the
door for the sake of air, a sudden clamour of voices arose outside.
Then a thudding noise, — the gathering of a bare-footed crowd.
We turned out into the scorching sun to where, in the centre of the
arid waterside space, a fight was in progress. A policeman, buttoned
up in a blue linen uniform like a butcher-boy's coat, only double-
breasted, was struggling with a big-headed negro. The captive had
hold of his captor's cocomacaque club, and the pair swung to and
fro in a heated struggle.

The big-headed negro was already wresting away the weapon
when two other policemen raced up. Smash went a cocomacaquc
on the big, stooping head, and a bubble of red blood rose through
the short fuzz. A bellow of excitement went up from the bystanders.
The prisoner turned like a dazed bull for a moment, then he broke
free and fled down the street.

Experience soon taught me that similar scenes were by no means uncommon: I also learnt to sympathise with the frantic resistance of the prisoners.

The business in Jacmel is almost entirely in the hands of the small foreign element. The Republican Government distrusts and dislikes the outlander, but it cannot get on without him. On sufferance therefore he remains, but any projects as to opening up the country, prospecting or obtaining concessions, are blocked in one way or another. Either the Government plants its foot firmly and refuses permission point-blank, or if expediency suggests another course, negotiations are begun, which are later on so craftily manipulated that the white man finds himself finally left in the lurch, saddled with a hopelessly bad bargain.

Again no foreigner can legally own land in the island, but so far as private houses in the coast towns are concerned, this law has been circumvented at various times.

There are in the town and district about 500 potential soldiers, of whom no fewer than 200 are generals. A general, as he is known in Hayti, must be spelt with a big G. The general commanding this province is one of the strong men of the country. He can neither read nor write, and belongs to the lowest strata, yet he was one of the great forces in the last revolution. General Johannis Merisier cannot sign documents, but by way of making his mark he adds the impress of his signet ring. What one man writes for him he gets another man to read, thus securing himself against deception. In person he is of the ultranegro type, and in his hands lies the power of life and death.

Towards evening I went for a ride about the surrounding country ; there were some pretty-looking villas half hidden in green dotted about the outskirts of the town. Returning I passed by the arsenal under the walls of which public executions take place. Not so long ago two criminals, a man and a boy of fourteen (the latter had split open the paternal skull with a hatchet) were condemned to be shot. Upon the moment of firing a Roman Catholic priest went up to the boy and asked him if he repented of his crime. The boy said "No" — he would do it again if he had the chance.

"If you repent you will be reprieved."

"I do not repent."

The priest withdrew, and the twenty assorted firearms spoke. The man fell upon his knees, but the boy was untouched. The volley rang out again. No result. Another volley. The bleeding man pitched forward dead, but the boy stood in the aching sunlight, still unhurt.

A general rode up, and borrowing a cocomacaque from a by-stander, beat the soldiers over the head for their bungling. He swore that unless the next attempt took effect, the men themselves should be shot. A second later, the boy fell riddled with bullets. Then the drums beat, for the justice of the Republic was satisfied. On this occasion it was said that the soldiers had pity on the youth of the boy, and purposely shot wide, each man hoping that his comrade's bullet might do the deed. But it was a cruel mercy.

Darkness had come on by the time I recrossed the market-place. The scene was weird. Among the ruinous wooden booths a few fluttering flames cut into the blackness of the night, and from the gloom around came the indescribable screeching babble of negro voices. Here and there in the dim light I saw pale-palmed hands twisting in gesticulation, or wide mouths that flashed white teeth over slips of sugar-cane. And so the busy unseen night-life, which the dark-skin loves, went on under the dense sky.

2

The High Road of Hayti

LIBERTY, EQUALITY, FRATERNITY.
Permit to the Citizen Petit Saiis-Nom (Little Nameless),
mounted on a red mule bearing the brand S.S., to go to Port-au-
Prince as guide to Monsieur Plesketh Prichard, an English subject.
Request to the Authorities, Civil and Military, to render to him
any aid or protection of which he may stand in need.

Jacmel, 22 November, 1S99.

This passport, (of which the original is in French) signed and
stamped with the round blue stamp of the Communal Council of
Jacmel, made me free of some seventy miles of the chief high road
of Hayti, lying between the port of Jacmel and the capital. Along it
mails and money pass every fortnight by the agency of couriers and
mules. Outside of Hayti this road bears a sinister reputation. To
quote from a letter written to me from a neighbouring island: "
Persons may travel with great danger by land over the hills from
Jacmel to Port-au-Prince."

The country lying between is said to be a hotbed of snake-worship, with its accompaniments of superstition and sacrifice, as, indeed, is all the mountain-land of the Republic.

On first sight, my guide, Petit Sans-Nom, was a puny Haytian of meek aspect. His duty in life was to clean out the Custom House, with interludes of acting as courier on the Port-au-Prince road. His face and head were curiously small, and he wore a scanty curling goatee. In his soiled white coat and ragged trousers he listened humbly while the General of the Custom House was good enough to say that if he misbehaved himself he should, on any complaint from me, be immediately cast into prison. I left him pursuing his vocation with a grass broom.

On the morrow we met again. His bearing was surprisingly altered ; a heavy cutlass swung at his side, and he was fiercely urging a little mule to the appointed starting-place. Two grass bags were slung across the mule, into which he stowed my baggage, and while one wondered how so undersized an animal could be expected to carry it. Petit Sans-Nom, perceiving that the two sides did not balance, considerately added an enormous stone as a makeweight. He then mounted on top of all, and sat awaiting my convenience in the shade of a tamarind tree. Five minutes afterwards I had bidden good-bye to H.B.M.'s

Consular Agent, to whose kindness I owed so much, and was riding with my guide out of Jacmel, I had been told that it would be necessary to ford the two rivers, the Grande Riviere and the Gosseleine, any number of times between a hundred and fifty and two hundred. Rain had also fallen recently, and the fords were deep. For a mile or so we threaded along the narrow track overhung by creepers and trees, and we were at the first ford.

The silver river, embedded in green and as clear as a trout stream, came suddenly across our way in one of its many bends. The water was about four feet deep, and the hour at which we crossed it was half-past three. Before the quarter to four I had counted nine fordages. By halfpast five the number had swelled to eighty-one. After that counting became monotonous. The road was, in fact, the river-bed, with its loops and oval curvings, and we followed it glen by glen through hollows clothed in fresh, rain-flushed greenery. Sometimes we sagged up and down hillsides, with now and then a glimpse upwards of a treeless, conical slope covered with pointed grey stones, or an open valley massed with foliage of a dark potato-leaf tint, flecked with the broad pale blades of banana palms.

Dusk came upon us while we were still making our way through the thickly-wooded gorges; the river-bed, (considered as a high road) becoming worse every moment.

Fireflies came out and danced among the foliage overhead, and all the myriad crickets and frogs ticked and croaked about us, like an army of pigmies marking time. We had arranged to sleep at the foot of the mountains, and my guide had promised that we should arrive there before nightfall.

When darkness unmistakably settled down, I asked him how much farther we had to go. Petit Sans-Nom stooped to no subterfuge. "Far, far," he said, frankly. And far it was. Hour joined hour in the measureless past, and still we struggled on. At this stage of the journey we began to pass human habitations which in every particular might have been borrowed wholesale from West Africa. Here and there red fires burned in the gloom of a stockade. Round them crouched figures clad in little, the children clad not at all, and in the heart of the glow were people dancing to the monotonous clap of hands. Outside the circle you could see the squat outlines and the humpy shoulders of thatch huts.

MY GUIDE.

At last the small mule mutinied. She refused to face a ford, and tipped off the baggage and Petit Sans-Nom with one abrupt action. She submitted to the baggage being loaded on again, but allow her human burden to remount she would not. So the procession of two became a procession of three, the guide straining on the head-rope, the mule throwing off the baggage whenever possible, and the traveller and horse bringing up a weary and inglorious rear.

The prospect of sleep and food receded while the hours went by, but, as my horse gathered himself to scramble up a steep bank of more than usual slipperiness. Petit Sans-Nom encouraged him with the remark that it was the last ford, and rising above us in the gloom I made out the dim shoulder of a mountain. With renewed hope we climbed upwards into a sound of voices singing. A palm-thatched hut peeped through the foliage, and in it they were holding high festival. Petit Sans-Nom pulled down the gate of the enclosure, and led the way in, and by the starlight I saw two or three subsidiary huts beside the one where they were making merry. The guide shouted, and the noise ceased abruptly; the door opened, and questions were asked in Creole, to which we were able to give satisfactory replies. Forthwith they invited us inside.

There were six people in the central windowless room, which was lit by a flaming tin lamp that leaped in the draughts, and showed the earthen floor, wooden table, and red water-bottle, the ordinary furnishing of the peasant's home. A little girl was stirred to wakefulness, a tablecloth was produced, a mattress was laid upon the floor. I can remember eating something, and lying down. My next recollection is the being wakened some hours before daylight.

While it was still dark we ascended the lower spurs of the mountain, which rises eastward to Prince's Peak, 5,000ft. high, and the dawn was not full when we could see both grey seas, — to the south the Caribbean Sea, to the north the bay of Port-au-Prince, with its misty island.

The river road had been bad, but the mountain road was worse. When we met a cavalcade of donkeys we spent half an hour in edging across the top of a precipice, where the path only allowed of the passage of one at a time. When at last we reached the level, the track broadened out into a road some 30ft. wide, but horses and donkeys had passed over it when it was soft with the rains, and the sun had subsequently hardened the hollows and mouldings of mud into ridges. We followed this route across the plain through the forenoon until we came within sight of the sea which lay beyond a broad belt of swamp. A wind puffed lazily over the marsh, and the sun beat furiously down upon the road as we were swept up into a mile-long procession of negroes and negresses with laden donkeys and mules on their way to the morrow's market.

We came to a bridge after a while, and my guide said: "When you see a bridge always go round it." Later I discovered this to be a national proverb. It was sound advice, too, for the bridge had a 6ft. hole in the centre of it. Here the road, in spite of all its short-comings, was a highway, with its dark stream of people flowing ahead of us into the capital.

So with the sun still boring a hole in the small of my back, I at length jogged, wet and weary, into the heart of Port-au-Prince, where, after a little searching, I found a hotel.

They say that the first act of every nation in founding a new colony is typical. Spain builds a church, England founds a bank, and La Belle France opens and patronises a cafe. For the moment, I preferred the French plan in that it administers to the primary necessities of the human frame.

France has evacuated Port-au-Prince for a hundred years; do her cafes survive? In a degenerate form they do, for Haytian life is negro life grafted upon French life, and the black man possesses among his faults or virtues a strong conservatism. The national impulse of the colonising Frenchman is to imitate Paris. The nearer his handiwork can approach to the original ideal, the nearer he is to bliss.

We have, therefore, in the town of Port-au-Prince an imitation of Paris made a hundred years ago by men who had seen the original; and carried on and revised during the last century by a negro race, who — the enormous majority of them, at least — have not.

MARKET-PLACE, PORT-AU-PRINCE.

The hotel to which I had come was an oblong building, rimmed below with narrow doors, and above with the usual wooden piazza. Mules and horses were hitched to the posts, and from the open doors an overpowering smell of coffee greeted you. The bar was filled with Haytians, many in black frock-coats and straw hats, imbibing the brown "rhum" of the country.

They were lean men, bony-shouldered, with long faces pointed by fuzzy thin goatees, who greeted each other with an elaborate politeness, shaking hands indifferently with the right hand or the left.

The coloured barman manipulated a long drink, and the question of a room in which to sleep was mooted. Had they one? Had they not! a fine big room, would *le blanc* engage? No, *le blanc* would see first. Would *le blanc* come this way then, and they would show him? He followed, and, passing through a dining-room of five or six tables, furnished with dirty cloths and picturesque red earthenware water-jugs, was once more in the street.

Turning to the left, we found an iron door on which the ancient red paint was blotched and faded. It opened upon a basement crowded with dogs and negroes; from this a wooden staircase climbed to the upper floor of the establishment. The building was two rooms thick. First came the ante-room and billiard-room, and here the afternoon heat hung palpable. A wine-splashed table gave the place an air of just awaking after a night of it, and the idea was not refuted by after-experience. Then on along a black passage to No. 9, and I was there.

The room had been but lately vacated, and the evidence of another presence spoke aloud from bed and basin. Two windows gave upon the street, further ventilation was provided by jalousies opening into the sleeping rooms on each side, lack of privacy being a detail compared with the luxury of a thorough draught. A mosquito-net of bygone efficacy hung stagnant over the bed, and mosquitoes buzzed round the dirty wooden walls in platoons.

This was the room, the waiter could not conceal his pride in it — a fine room, as one could see; would not *le blanc* engage?

To whom did this hotel belong, — to a Haytian? But yes, to a Haytian certainly. The rent of the room was two dollars per day. Monsieur would stay *en pension*" That would be two dollars more. Thus, for the sum of four dollars a day (Haytian value), drinks extra, the wanderer in Hayti had secured a resting-place and stokerage.

Outside the windows coursed an open drain which told plainly of its mission, and refuse of all indescribable sorts lay inches deep in the street. The view extended over the lower town, beyond which stood up the tall masts of ships; farther still, the green, nameless islands of Port-au-Prince Bay set against a background of blue tropic sea. How the heat danced! And the noises in the street, — the uncouth yelling of negroes, the bark of dogs, and the grunt of scavenging pigs, — came up in a babel.

What with the heat, the mosquitoes, and the noise there arose a yearning for that primary necessity — a bath. The heavy-footed negro came padding back into the room. The tin bath was at the service of *le blanc.* At once? He would see. And after that, something to eat. Very good! It was a first experience of the Haytian *garçon,* and things hung fire.

But to describe the first night in that room! No wind stirred the steaming air; it was like living at the bottom of a well of vapour. Cocks crowed throughout the livelong night, and poker was being played with vivacity at the end of the passage from which one was only divided by mere wooden slats. Not fifty odd miles in the saddle could conquer these drawbacks and bring the welcome gift of sleep.

Next morning *le blanc* turned up to *déjeuner* weary and heavy-eyed after a late morning sleep.

"Slept well?" asked an American, "any mosquitoes?" All visible skin-surfaces bore eloquent witness." Yes, by Josh! they've done you proud. Say, ever hear the story of the man who shot a mosquito up in that room of yours with an eight-bore duck gun, and only wounded it?"

For four days and nights I held the fort of No. 9, then I gave in, capitulated miserably, and left the mosquitoes and noises in possession. I departed towards evening, and the loose-treading, good-hearted nigger waiters, who sleep on three chairs, and don't know what a mosquito is, save by the sense of sight, came round and demanded " petits cadeaux."

After all, I left with some regret, for though the hotel was dirty, it must in fairness be said that one could meet with its equal in that respect in not a few places within the Spanish frontier. And, at least, the proprietors were amiably anxious to please, and spared no trouble.

I went up to the only other hotel in the town, which stands above the palace of the President on the Champ-deMars. There the arrangements accorded better with prejudiced English notions, and there was a night wind thrown in. It is difficult to realise that in the whole State, containing, it is said, some million and three-quarters of inhabitants, there exist but three hotels.

Occasionally when I was feeling low I used to go down and have a meal at my old quarters, and the thought that it was no longer my fate to become mosquito-chop in No. 9 never failed to throw a fresh luminance of relief over my sojourn in the capital of the Black Republic.

So for some weeks I sojourned in Port-au-Prince and by degrees acquired a knowledge of the Black Man's capital.

Within an arc of hazy blue mountains, threaded with clouds of a hundred delicate shades, Port-au-Prince lies upon its beaches like the white skeleton of a stranded whale, of which the rib-bones are the houses. The grass, that seems to grow between them, heads up into palm trees as you draw nearer. Viewed from afar you would call it one of the most beautiful spots on God's earth. But go down into the squalid streets, and you find the town is a fester, a scar made by man, as it were of malice prepense, upon the natural loveliness of his environment.

It was good on quiet evenings and on certain cloudy dawns to ride away from this city of gutters and garbage, out of earshot of the multiloquous negro voices, and look down on the blue horse-shoe of the bay, where the island of Gonave floats in shadow, and to watch the soft southern greys and purples thrown on mountain, shore, and sea.

At first sight Port-au-Prince looks fair enough to be worth travelling 5,000 miles to see; once enter it, and your next impulse is to travel 5,000 miles to get away again. Passing through the streets, the life around seems a strange graft of Parisianism and savagery. Here is an idolatry of fashion, an insistent militarism, and an exuberance of speech all verging on the grotesque — a distended caricature of the original.

Here the white man, as opposed to the black, has no rights worthy of the name. Moreover, the town is under martial law. This condition of things is permanent, although the country has been for several years past at rest from internal dissensions. After nine you are challenged in the streets, and at no time of the day or night are you out of sight of a soldier.

The chief boulevard is the Rue des Miracles, a broad street some three-quarters of a mile in length. Trees overhang the roadway, a wheezy steam-tram makes half-hourly journeys up and down from the quays to the Champ de Mars. There are no footways; road-mending appears to be a lost art, and the whole surface is as rough as the bed of a torrent.

At intervals of from 50 to 100 yards you find a post of soldiers. They live in ramshackle guardrooms made of wood turned rust-colour from lack of care and the corrosion of torrential rains, a longish hovel with the inevitable piazza raised some two feet above the street. Below flows an open drain. The heavy faces of the men are blotched with sleep. Some play dice on the bench by the wall, some lounge in hammocks slung from the trees over the sluggish sewer; two or three fires of boughs serve to cook their slender meals, which are not provided by the State. A collection of guns leans against the trees at various angles. The whole is more like a mid-forest bivouac of a few ragged blacks than a scene in the main thoroughfare of a capital.

The city has no architectural pretensions. The houses are mostly built of wood, and fires are of frequent occurrence, though it is now some time since they had a serious one. The finest buildings are the Cathedral, which stands at the head of the boulevard, and the white palace of the President. When I passed the latter the President was sitting on the balcony, playing draughts. He is a full-blooded negro, with a heavy face and huge negro mouth set between a grey beard and grey hair brushed up from his forehead. He must weigh close upon eighteen stone.

He is a superlative specimen of his race, and the black faction in Hayti have at least secured an admirably representative figurehead. To make this clear, it must be explained that Hayti for the black, as differentiated from the mulatto or coloured man, is the watchword of the great majority in the Republic.

The palace stands on the fringe of the Champ de Mars, where the reviews are held; — an open space, on which the scanty grass breaks into patches of dusty baldness, and bloated bull-frogs hold nightly concerts in the intersecting ditches.

Turning back to the city, one passes by the steps of the Cathedral, which is open and tropical, the interior hung with dark curtains and supplied with a profusion of pictures and colour. The town possesses a peculiar picturesqueness of its own, unlike anything one sees in any other quarter of the globe. But you walk through its cobbled streets with circumspection, for they are ankle-deep in refuse.

Even in the Place, which contains the Consulates and the chief shops, there is a heap of corruption five or six feet high and more than proportionately long. The waspish cab of the country, known as a "bus," has just about room to pass between this gigantic rubbish-shoot — or, as it might more truthfully be called, dunghill— and a black drain that skirts the beams supporting the piazzas of the houses. And this is the cleanest street in Port-au-Prince.

It is appalling to imagine what might happen were an epidemic to break out here. The town has its foundations literally set upon decay. I have seen more than one of those unhealthy spots to which is attached the sobriquet of "White Man's Grave," but none of them have the invitation to disease written so plainly across their faces as this city of Port-au-Prince. And yet disease in its largest sense seldom visits it.

At the corner of the Rue-du-Peuple I came upon a white man, clad in sea-going blue, moving cautiously with disgusted nostril.

"Hello!" he said; "would you be so good as to point out to me the shortest way to the quay?"

I indicated the direction,

" I say," he continued, overlooking me with interest, "how long have you lived here.'"

" Four days," I said.

"I wish I had your constitution then! I've been ashore here an hour and three-quarters, and if I haven't a museum of the most virulent microbes inside me it isn't the fault of this town, that's all." And he passed on hurriedly.

6 O'CLOCK REVEILLE IN THE STREETS OF PORT-AU-PRINCE.

PALMS ON THE WAY TO KENSCOFF.

It is about the filthiest place in the world; shut in by mountains from the cool north winds, it stews on from year to year in stagnant heat. No smallest effort is made at sanitation; the street-drains with all their contaminations flow down and help to fill up the harbour. At times the rain flushes them, and this effort of Nature seems to be the sole force that tends to cleanliness. Under these circumstances you would expect Port-au-Prince to pay a heavy toll to the lords of disease. Surely this must be the most unhealthy spot in the world. But it is not so. Why? There you have a question no one can answer.

Of course the ordinary malarial fevers are by no means uncommon, but the absence of other and more serious diseases leaves one to speculate to what height Port-au-Prince might soar as a health resort if an enterprising and wholesome Government did away with the present-day horrors of the streets.

Among this accumulated dirt, black ladies, in all cases well-dressed — many of them in the handiwork of Parisian artists — pick their perilous way or drive past in buggies atilt at impossible angles over the unevenness of the streets. Wherever you go the policeman, with his four-foot, ironshod club of cocomacaque, is a constant and conspicuous figure.

He demands a chapter to himself, but it is difficult to forego mention of him here, as his zeal is so significant a factor in the Haytian daily life. When he has fairly got his man down, and knocked most of the life out of him

with his club, the picture he makes standing over the bleeding figure in the road, with the ancient litter about them, and the blazing sun over all, could scarcely find its counterpart out of wild West Africa.

Passing under an arch bearing the name of a late President, "Hippolyte —President, Progress — Union," I entered the chief market, and it was market-day. The buyers and sellers spread themselves like an open camp into the streets around, the smell was appalling; and here, seated upon the leavings of bygone markets, the citizens of the Republic do a brisk trade.

The meat market is well supplied; it is presided over by burly butchers and gorged bluebottles. In the various approaches you can trace unpleasantly the evolution of flesh-foods, the raw material of your future meals. Pigs and goats, with their legs tied together, raise their voices in expostulation as they lie in the sun. One has wriggled to a neighbouring drain, and is gulping the thick fluid. Women, with piles of vegetables and fruit, boast one against the other; over the vociferous babble rises the lilt of a monotonous song. Fires smoulder here and there, and the acrid blue smoke hangs between sun and scene.

The whole is unique, Haytian; politeness is mingled with brutality, raucousness with a strange grace of demeanour. Picturesque, but eminently nasty, the spirit of neglect, one inevitable accompaniment of a black Government, broods over all, till one sickens in the sunshine.

"We are polite always," said a man to me. He spoke in vindication of various evils. But one cannot justify one's destiny by raising one's hat to a stranger.

Port-au-Prince leaves you with three impressions more vivid than the rest: the puny beasts of burden, each surmounted by a negress; the blue pervasive soldier, and the black pervasive dirt. Through the human torrent old hooded cabs are driven recklessly, and the open market is the backwash of the stream.

Just outside the town, towards the triumphal arch of Hippolyte, is a building with a roof of corrugated iron. You go in. The rude painting of a snake, a few soiled flags, a few prints from illustrated papers, are almost its sole furniture and ornament. You would not think it, but here you are in a Vaudoux temple, clinging upon the very skirts of civilisation. The worship is carried on, if not openly, at least unrestrainedly.

3

The Haytian General

Hayti is governed by Generals in all sizes. I wonder how many of them there are in the country. I wondered all the time I was there. I am still wondering. The General is so ubiquitous that it leads you to doubt whether it may not be possible that while to be a General is no compliment, not to be one is in the nature of a slap in the face.

I have been given the rank myself; given it by many, in the hot white street; given it by the drivers of wheezy, weedy fiacres, by goateed Haytian gentlemen —General, General. You could not, I am sure, walk along any of the main streets of Port-au-Prince without meeting ten Generals.

One day I tried to attract the attention of a small black boy who sometimes did odd jobs for me. His age I should put at ten years. A companion of his who saw my need

shouted across to attract his attention. What did he shout? Why — " Général."

I occupied myself for some time in looking up the numerical force of military Hayti. I could find no exact statistics of later data than 1867, when there were 6,500 Generals of Division, 7,000 regimental officers, and 6,500 privates. At this computation the troops commanded by each General of Division consisted of one private and one regimental officer, and one-thirteenth of a regimental officer.

I made a great many inquiries as to the army of the Republic, I tapped a hundred possible sources of information, but found no one able to supply me with hard, sure, and certain facts on the subject. Like Hadji Baba of immortal memory, when he was sent to discover the number of the enemy's guns, they were wont to make answer in the same illusory fashion, "One — two — three — five —six hundred."

At length in a fortunate hour I purchased of an ancient man a book which purported to give a list of the regiments and some other details. I took it to one of the officials, who I supposed might be able to help me, and asked him if it was correct. He loosely said it was. Anyway, it was not hopelessly incorrect, and he added that if I secured the exact statistics for the moment I should probably find them considerably modified in six months. There is evidently no stagnation of this particular kind in Hayti.

As I have said, the country is governed by Generals. The biggest of all is President Tiresias Augustin Simon Sam. Directly under him are the Generals of Departments ; below them are Generals of Arrondissements and of Communes. Lower again are Generals of subdivisions, Generals of Postes Militaires, and so it goes on. There is a General of the prison, and a General of the women's prison.

The man who kept the hotel I stayed at was not a General, but then he was not a Haytian. At last I found myself asking whether the waiter did not, on his evenings off, also flower into a lace-bound General. There have been waiters very much Generals, and one who made himself not only a General-President, but a General-Emperor.

It is beautiful, this militarism, but it has made me decide never to return to Hayti. Baptiste of the soda-water syphon, who nightly waged war with the little boys under the door-slats, might in the meantime have become a General, and who can say in what spirit he might remember the former exactions of the white man?

The General is prolific; not that I mean that all his sons are Generals "ipso facto," but from the forcing-ground of each revolution springs a new crop of honours. What could be cheaper for the exchequer or more gratifying to the individual than the bestowal broadcast of the rank of General!

They say, but this 1 do not guarantee, that a certain President beat a man at a game of draughts, and in his delight immediately presented him with a General 's commission. There is only one thing of which I am absolutely certain, which is, that they will not make me a General for writing all this about them.

Lesser titles are very small potatoes indeed — " Aut General aut nullus." But when you look a little more closely, while still criticising in the friendliest spirit, you cannot help wondering if this elevation in the bulk to high military rank is not due to the same spirit as that which impels the savage to clothe himself in the rather quaint combination of a tall hat and a girdle of hearse feathers.

The same tendency towards display led in the year 1849 to the creation of a black nobility. At that time Soulouque was Emperor, calling himself Faustin the First, and he showered titles with a lavish hand among his supporters. Black dukes and barons strutted it through the Court. The Emperor gave the titles, but left it to the favoured ones to choose their own designations, which they apparently did more according to sound than to knowledge.

Of the four Princes one was Bobo, and it is almost tragic to learn that among the fifty-nine dukes were their Graces of Marmalade and Lemonade! But Mr. James Anthony Fronde's allusion to dukes and marquises driving over the white man in the streets of Port-au-Prince as late as 1887 is surely something of an anachronism, like certain other of the same gentleman's statements.

To-day their places are taken by Generals. The Haytian is tender upon the subject of their multiplicity. If you ask him questions concerning the swollen list he grows restless and prefers another topic. In Hayti they are always conjugating a compound verb. They begin young — in the future tense: "I will be a General." Everyone hankers to be a General. It is the hall-mark of success. He to whom success comes vaunts himself, " I am a General of the Republic" ; and the conjugation has rather often been known to end abruptly in the past tense: "He was a General." The man who lives to say the last of himself says it from overseas, coupled with bitter reflections upon his native land.

An urban General is in most cases but a name, whereas his congener of the country is usually a living power. You find in the villages that the General of place and commune has a distinct position. He lives in a house a little larger and a little better than those of his neighbours — I had almost said subjects — with an extra outbuilding in his stockade, a better horse, and, perhaps, an extra wife or two. Under his fierce rule the commune bows to the rigour of the law; the peasantry cannot be said to prosper, but at least they are inoffensive and polite.

The reason is not far to seek. The black man can no more govern his black brother successfully without tyranny than you can reach a blind man's sense without touch or speech. No appeal is made to his reason ; he is coerced by solid fear.

Hear him pray, and you will understand him better. He does not supplicate his God ; he demands of his God ; he essays to bargain. That is because his deity is far away out of sight; therefore, in relation to that unfelt power he begins to esteem himself and his desires, and to be puffed up out of all due proportion. Whereas the grip of his General's iron hand is unmistakably evident over all the hours of his daily life.

When I was at Thomazeau, the last Haytian town before one reaches the Dominican frontier, an incident very typical of the Spartan sway of these local pashas had occurred. A man stole a cow. He was caught and shot dead the next morning by orders of the General de la Place. The result of this measure of summary justice was that you might have left a handful of silver dollars — nay, more, your open rum flask — in the village street, nor would any man have dared to help himself to either. But these Generals, with substantive power, are conspicuously in the minority.

Regarded from the point of view of possible leaders of the Haytian army, it must be conceded that they have yet to prove their significance and to win their spurs. Since the war with San Domingo, in which no reputations were made, the Haytian Generals have not led the troops down to alien battle. They have contented themselves with being up to the hilt in revolutions, and with sunning themselves at dusty reviews.

If, however, the State ever calls them to its service, it is unlikely that the troops will be left without a General. Hayti calculates to throw at any moment 8,000 men into the field, and of these only a smattering would not be full Generals.

It may be thought it is because of the emoluments that the Haytian likes to become a General, but the State is wiser than that ; out of the numbers who are entitled to wear gold lace not one in ten ever sees the colour of State money. Each subsists as he can, yet clings to the nominal honour, although it brings many expenses in its train. A story goes that the Haytian, while quite content to leave his all of worldly wealth behind him, yet hopes to bear with him his rank of General across the lonely frontier, and still to cut a figure with it in another and a better world.

But let us proceed to consider the Soldier. My first speaking acquaintance with him occurred one night on the Champ-de-Mars near the President's Palace. I repeated the conversation with little variation on numerous occasions afterwards.

"*Blanc*, I am a soldier, give me ten centimes."

" You have your pay."

" My General has taken my pay. I am a poor man and a soldier. Give me ten centimes."

"How long have you been a soldier?"

"Three years."

"When did you have your pay last?"

" Very long ago, and I am hungry. Give me ten centimes. Merci, *blanc*."

He stood before me, with his chinless, thick-lipped black face under a blue cap banded with red. He wore dried grass slippers, shabby tweed trousers, and a faded light-blue coat. Over his shoulders by a rough hemp rope was slung a flintlock gun, and he was hurrying towards beat of drum to fall in for the evening parade. At half-past five p.m. the bugle-calls come trickling through the crowded streets, drums beat, and the army of Hayti arises from its benches and its dice. The guard at the houses of Ministers and the men at the police-stations gather together, shoulder arms, and line up by fours to twenties.

Their officer stands in front of them with a drawn rusty sword. The soldiers continue to be interested in their individual concerns. One is chewing a banana, another is wolfing sugar-cane, gnawing doglike at a piece two feet long. They stand there, very much at ease, for about twenty minutes, occasionally going through a slovenly series of movements, then the General takes himself off, and the Haytian army once more disposes itself on its benches and dozes if it is more than usually hungry.

Of course each regiment has a uniform of its own, but the soldiery, save on review days — of which more anon — put on the trousers the good God sends them and are thankful. Of a score drawn up in line no two are dressed alike; their workaday uniform is limited to the red-banded kepi and rags. As to weapons, a broken bristle of bayonets sticks up along the file, but all the men have rifles. They are of different calibres and decades — almost, one might say, of different centuries. In one group I found a decrepit magazine, a flintlock, and a self respecting Remington.

A GENERAL'S EVENING RIDE.

The State does not undertake any commissariat obligations, and the private's pay trickles down to him through more than one absorbent channel. Visible means of subsistence he has practically none; he seeks food to eke out existence much as a stray cat does in England. He purrs pitifully and pessimistically about the '*blanc*' when he meets him, and pounces upon the weaker units of his own colour with a highly-developed instinct of plunder. When there happens to be a lack of such happy chances and he is more than usually hungry, he goes to sleep. So in the hot town the Haytian soldiery drowses unstirred by dreams of golden glory. Its attention is fully occupied in strenuous effort to keep its stomach full. At the worst it does odd jobs and carries coffee-sacks.

Every third man you meet is a General; only every tenth General, as I have said before, gets paid, but every General tries to pay himself. The pay of these personages is nominally -£140 per amum for a General of Division, and £105 for a Brigadier! The sums grow less in ratio to the rank: a Captain is given a competency of £12, and the Private wallows in the wild prodigality of about £2 10s a year — and that not always forthcoming.

When you know how the Haytian soldier is paid, you know how Hayti is governed. The principle is one and indivisible. The paymaster takes toll of the 50 centimes and passes it on to the fir.st General. The first General, who is a very big General indeed, hands it on in slimmer bulk to the second General. He in his turn transfers it, further diminished, to his next in command. The Captain lightens it lest it should be too heavy for the Lieutenant to carry, and the Lieutenant, not liking to break the chain takes his own discount ; thus the soldier who receives five centimes is in luck ; he who gets ten is a favourite of the gods. And when at last he has pocketed it, his Lieutenant comes along and wins it off him at the universal game of dice.

This sounds very grotesque, but it is none the less sober truth. Nor is it a matter of isolated instances; it happens every week as regularly as pay-day comes, and will in all probability go on happening every week as long as the Black Republic endures.

"Big fleas have little fleas upon their backs to bite 'em, " so we say, but Hayti, as her custom is, twists the order round, for the smallest flea is the soldier, and upon him feed a whole series of larger fleas.

There are more ways than one of extracting sustenance out of him, as witness the following case which occurred quite recently. A countrywoman brought into market the best yield of her plantation. By sale and barter she accumulated a good store of provisions, and, being feeble, hired a sample of the ubiquitous soldier to carry her possessions to her mules some half-a-mile away. The soldier walked in front of her, and all went well until she met an acquaintance in the street and stopped to exchange gossip. The old lady was interested, and the soldier, for once finding himself able to nip a smaller flea than himself, seized the opportunity to decamp to his arrondissement with the loot.

On arrival he awoke his sleeping comrades, others left off gambling for the moment at the rare prospect of food, and the whole guard set to work to divide the spoil and to put the butter, the pork, and the rum beyond the reach of their original owner. But while they were engaged in tearing open the second tin of butter, the Lieutenant of the post hove in sight. Now when an officer sees a soldier with a sufficiency of provisions he naturally jumps to the conclusion that they must have been stolen; therefore the Lieutenant, having listened to two minutes of fluent lying, went off posthaste to acquaint the General next above him with the condition of affairs.

This General was a prompt man. He lost no time in committing the Lieutenant to prison for not having appropriated the food and brought it at once to him. Then he got a horse, galloped down to the post, sent the guard off to jail in bulk, and carried the whole plunder to his own house. But, unluckily for that energetic individual, the story got abroad, and a certain still more highly placed black General despatched a message to say that the butter, rum and pork would be just as safe under his care as anywhere else. Such hints from a superior in Hayti are, like royal invitations, not to be refused.

The peasant woman returned home empty, the soldier gained a few mouthfuls of food and prison, the Lieutenant prison only; the first General gained the sense of complacency consequent on possession for the space of an hour, while the biggest flea of all pouched the booty that had come up the long military ladder to enrich one of the highest in the land. There can be no doubt if the old lady ever applies for her own (which is unlikely) she will also be put into prison for losing it.

There is no conscription, and the battalions are recruited, not by any regular enforcement of law, but by a system of press-gangs armed with the cocomacaque. A young English subject, black, about eighteen years old, was impressed in this manner recently. He objected on the ground of his nationality, but the recruiting party cared not at all for that, and, after beating him, flung him into jail. He was of course released on the representations of his Consul.

There is another evil which pervades the army, and that is the influence of the Papaloi. At Vaudoux sacrifices the soldier class is always well represented. This statement is not upon hearsay evidence. I have seen a general in uniform kill a cock in honour of the sacred snake under the eyes of a large number of worshippers. If ever it should come to pass that the Papaloi were to order one thing and the authorities another, the average soldier would be extremely likely to disregard the wishes of the Government. He objects to a clubbing exceedingly, but he objects even more strongly to brave the wrath and vengeance of the unseen powers of darkness, whose representatives upon earth he believes the Vaudoux priests to be.

It is this prevalence of the Vaudoux sect which astonishes you. A priestess once boasted that if she beat the sacred drum in the centre of the town of Port-au-Prince, few even of the highest in the land would dare to disregard the summons. And you must own that when the third part of the spectators of the ceremonies is made up of negroes wearing the kepi, it is not unlikely that the boast of the priestess had good foundation as regards the army.

The tendency of the soldiery towards these horrible and grotesque superstitions is one of the safeguards of the votaries from punishment. You may set a thief to catch a thief if the first thief has any interest in so doing, but is it not absurd to expect to stamp out snake-worship by the agency of snake-worshippers, whom instinct inevitably throws back upon the primal religions?

THE MARCH PAST.

Nevertheless, although the Haytian becomes a soldier in spite of himself, and is heavily handicapped by circumstances, he is astonishingly free of one serious fault. He may be on occasion a bully and a thief, but he is not a drunkard, although he could get cheaply and comfortably drunk on tafia for two centimes. With steady handling he could be turned out a first-class fighting man; as he is, however, he can hardly be deemed an effective. Yet the opinion in many

Haytian circles is that it would be a bad day for any European force when it came in the way of the Republican troops.

"They would fight like heroes," said a General to me, "these brave ones! If any attacking army landed in this free Republic, they would without doubt instantly drive it into the sea."

On the first Sunday of each month a review is held on the Champ-de-Mars. On the particular Sunday when I had the luck to be present, it was to be an even grander review than usual, one of the events of the year. The earliest

intimation of the great doings came from the National Musical Company, whose martial strains drifted across in the glow of the morning, and I turned out to see what was going on.

The dusty Champ-de-Mars, with its fringe of white houses, its meandering drains, and its extensive prospect over calm waters, was just greeting the rising sun. The dew was yet wet upon the grass, the air was growing hotter with each moment. Beneath us the town was spread out in a chess-board of white and green, and afar off a few ships swung at anchor in the fjord-like bay.

Distant bugle calls tinkled like echoes from various points, a couple of Generals met together under a tree, and soon dark columns of soldiers began to crawl out from the town below. As they drew nearer I saw that they were changed from the men I knew. On week-days they lounge about the streets in ragged unkemptness, but on review days they blossom out into uniforms of gorgeous colours. Busy black Generals caracoled ostentatiously upon their flanks and in front of them, as they marched on to the field and formed into a hollow square. The town was now stirring like an ant-heap, and giving forth a broad stream of people on foot and in carriages.

Every scene has its dominant note, that aspect which first strikes the eye and afterwards lingers longest in the memory. Here it was struck by the negro Generals. There were three hundred of them at the least. Pink Generals, green Generals, blue Generals, and

Generals clad in the paler Cambridge tint; the plain was stiff with generals, score upon score, important, imposing, each in a web of gold lace, each mounted upon a small, long-tailed but excellent horse, each riding well, though after the splayfooted fashion of his race, each aware that the eyes of the world were upon him, and each determined upon keeping them fixed there.

They galloped hither and thither across the open square, they ambled along the ranks, they impressed themselves obtrusively upon the attention. To be a General it is not necessary ever to have been a soldier or officer of lesser rank, the title being bestowed for political purposes or, as an article of the Haytian Constitution has it, "for eminent services rendered to the State."

The assembled troops numbered perhaps 2,000, and I judged, from the diversity of equipment, that many of the thirty-eight regiments of the Republic were represented amongst them. There was a fine show of colour, although there were also deficiencies in the matter of foot-gear and rifles. Not a man of them all stood straight; they might have been galvanised figures jerked into position by some malignantly humorous intelligence. Yet you knew it was a great occasion, for not one individual was eating sugar cane, a height to which discipline rarely soars.

A bugle gave notice of developments. Generals smoothed down projecting angles with their horses as, riding swiftly, General St. Fort Colin, the Minister of War, curveted out into the golden sunshine. He galloped round, a word here, a sign there, and even as he finished his tour of inspection the music of the palace band heralded the approach of His Excellency General Tiresias Augustin Simon Sam, President of the Republic.

The palace band moved forward playing, and wonderfully well they played, and looked well, too, in red and blue and gold, with crested caps. After them came the President and his staff, sixty of them, Generals all.

They rode out into the Champ-de-Mars and cantered round, saluted and saluting. General Sam was in uniform, and his charger was caparisoned with a saddle-cloth of crimson and gold. He rides well, and has a soldierly bearing. He looked not only the head of the army, but the most soldier-like man in it, as he drew up under the shade of some trees and his staff wheeled into line behind him.

Then the march past began, led off by the National Musical Company. First the infantry, men in red trousers with black kits and red blankets, their band following; squads with blue jackets and red-tasseled caps, contingents more or less numerous in various blends of pink and green, blue and red, with touches of yellow in stripe or cord or tassel.

The artillery passed, a battery of five guns and a Nordenfeldt, each drawn by a single mule. Occasionally an aide-de-camp received an order and galloped away with it. Three or four times a standard-bearer was manoeuvred into place by a vociferous General. Once a woman with a basket of linen on her head was hunted off the ground by another General in light green.

Two regiments of cavalry belonging to the bodyguard filed by, each perhaps 200 strong, the first in gleaming brass helmets, the second chasseurs in blue. So it went on, colour after colour. General after General.

Little can be said as to the deportment of the troops. They marched in step to a certain degree, but the files lolloped past in a loose-backed zigzag that would have broken the heart of a drill sergeant. Yet, untrained and unstiffened as it was, there could be no doubt but that the right material was there, if it could be put into efficient hands.

The populace was, however, pleased with the performance, and greeted the appearance of the different regiments with that singular Oho which is the Haytian exclamation of approval ; with it he welcomes everything, from a lady who is fortunate enough to please his critical eye, to a cab accident in the street.

Few of the regiments exhibited their nominal strength of 250. This is no new failing. For many a day after the last war they were engaged in against San Domingo, the President of the period was wont to say to any stranger who remarked upon these depleted battalions: "Ah! they suffered much in the last war!" in a tone which gave the hearer to understand that he was looking upon the survivors of a later Balaclava, fought out desperately among the wooded tropic hills.

But tradition has it that the only people those heroes shot in any number were their own officers, at the orders of the then Emperor Soulouque, who, to excuse himself when vanquished by the Dominicans, accused his staff in bulk of having betrayed him, the army, and their country.

Hayti supposes herself to have modelled her army upon that of France, only in this, as in all other things she is a caricature rather than a copy of the original. She overdoes all her effects; she is like the *nouveau riche* who bought an old oak balustrade and had it overlaid with gold-leaf.

At length the last General of all the Generals had saluted, and the columns filed away into smallness down the road ; the President and his staff trotted back to the palace near by ; the grand review was over ; and I was left to reflect upon the fact that Hayti is the most unconditionally military State in the world, and that she makes no account of anything beneath the rank of General.

The Haytian, in spite of his huge pretensions, is, however, not naturally a soldier. Drill and discipline and the art of war are mere empty sounds to his ear. From his point of view they are entirely beside the question. What he cares for is to play at being a soldier ; he loves the accoutrement, the uniforms, the gold lace — especially the gold lace. He has a passion for military titles, military bombast, military display. Even on his postage stamp a cannon sprawls menacingly in front of his crossed flags ; but there it ends.

He brags perpetually of his patriotic determination to defend the last inch of his native land from the usurpation of the alien, yet he allows his neighbour, San Domingo, to push the frontier between the States farther and farther to the westward without offering the smallest effective objection.

The following is an attempt to reproduce a conversation between an Englishman and a trio of generals after the review.

Scene. The piazza of a palm-thatched hut in the hot tropic evening. The open space in front represents the village street. It breaks up at once beyond the huts into a straggling, loose-edged bridle path, which glints in the oblique light of the rising moon until it disappears into the forest.

Dark figures move to and fro in the half-dusk outside, and crowing cocks, the sound of horses making a meal off guinea-grass, the patter of donkeys, disturb the silence of the night. Three consequential Haytians in blue, green, and pink, thickly netted over with gold lace, are seated smoking. Also an Englishman. Mosquitoes, dust, sandflies, and a smell of coffee mixed with rank tobacco smoke temper the sweetness of the air.

Haytian (in blue uniform): "Général."

The other two: "Qui, mon Général."

Blue General (stretching): "I am tired. But the review of to-day — what a great spectacle!"

Pink General: " Oho! Assuredly, a great spectacle!"

Green General; "Without question the most magnificent spectacle that one can see."

Englishman: "I was much interested."

Blue G: "Our army is composed of brave men. The troops are the finest in the world! Do you not think so, monsieur?"

E, (choosing his words): "I have seen none like it."

Pink G. (who is fat, with streaks of yellow on the bulging whites of his eyes): "The tenue, the discipline of the men was admirable!"

Green G.: "The army of Hayti is one which reflects credit upon its officers. An army without officers — what is it? "

Blue G.: "Nothing, absolutely nothing!"

Pink G.: "The army of Hayti has never been conquered! The French were here: we drove them out! The English fought with us; where are they? But we — we — we are here always! We have never been conquered!"

Blue G.: "It would be impossible. We could not survive it."

Chorus: "It is true, my General, for in that case we should be dead!"

Blue G.: "But the Boers will conquer the English."

Pink and Green G's. (together) : " Yes, yes, Ladysmith has fallen. The Boers have captured the town."

E.: "Indeed? When?"

Blue G.: "To-day or to-morrow — it goes without saying."

E. (with relief): "Quite so."

Blue General (puffing out his chest): "The Boers and we Haytians are brothers. We also have fought for the independence of our country. They are a bad people, these English."

Pink G. (looking at the E.): "The *blanc* is perhaps an Englishman."

Green G.: "The blanc is an American."

Blue G.: "Yes, yes, an American. I have always said so."

E.: "Pardon, Generals, English."

Blue G. (with assurance): "Yes, yes, English, have I not said so?"

E.: "I am sorry to find, General, that you are on the side of the Boers."

Blue G. (shaking his fat black cheeks in vehement declamation): "What would you, monsieur? They are our brothers, these Bo-o-ers ! If I were fighting for them! — But, no, I am here. The white English, they would crush the Bo-o-ers ! "

Chorus: "But they cannot! Vive les brave Bo-o-ers!"

E: "The Boers are white also, messieurs."

Blue G. (not to be taken in) : " No, no, they are not white."

E. : "I assure you — "

Blue G.: "The Boers live in Africa. All who live in Africa, excepting the English, are black men." (The General who made this astounding statement was an ex-Minister of War.)

Chorus: "'It is true."

K.: " On the contrary, if you will pardon my presumption in mentioning the fact, the Boers are, undoubtedly, white. They came from Europe in the first place, and took the land from the Africans. Now the English are taking the land from the Boers."

Blue General: " The English are brave men. I say so! They are the bravest men in the world. The Haytians conquered them. My regiment — " (At this moment a bugle call resounds in the village street, a commotion is to be observed in the military arrondisse-ment opposite. A short score of ragged negroes in light- blue coats, and trousers the worse for wear, tumble lazily out and form up in irregular line before a short, goateed black with a little sword.)

Pink G.: " Monsieur, see, the soldiers of the Republic."

E.: "How many men such as these could his Excellency the President put into the field at a week's notice?"

Pink G.: "Twenty-five thousand!"

E.: "An army indeed! How many troops were present today at the review on the Champ de Mars?"

Blue G. (not to be behindhand): "Ten thousand." (At the outside there were hardly i,8oo.)

Pink G.: "I was there."

E.: "I observed you there. General. Your horse — "

Pink G.: ' My horse? Oho! that is a horse! He can go a hundred miles a day."

Blue G. (cutting in): " President Sam is the father of the army. He is undertaking reforms which will make our army the equal of the first armies in Europe. Such men as ours — as you saw to-day, monsieur — can do anything. When all is ready we will drive the Dominicans into the sea, and the whole island shall be ours!"

Chorus: "Vive la Republique."

Blue G.: " When all is ready we will send officers to Europe to show the French, the Germans, and the English what an officer can attain to."

Pink G.: "I will then go to Europe."

Blue G. (with excitement): " Oho! It is I who will go! I have already been chosen. I am of the cavalry."

E. (hurriedly in the uproar): "During the last revolution — "

Pink G. (asserting himself): "If a revolution were to break out I would proceed at once to the place and put a stop to it."

Blue G. (with quivering cheeks): " I also am not afraid of a revolution."

All (clapping their hands to their swords): "Who is afraid?"

Blue G.: "Fear? I do not know what it is!"

Pink G.: "I have never been afraid. And you, monsieur?"

E.: "I have been afraid very often."

Green G.: "If you feel afraid, talk! It will do you good."

E.: "Having seen the Grand Review to-day, I should like to hear more about the Haytian forces. Will you be good enough to tell me something- of interest?"

Pink G. (after a moment's deep thought): "I am General of Division."

E. (who has heard it rumoured that Generals outnumber privates in the Haytian army, wishes to set the question at rest): "How many men are in your command?"

Pink G. (shrugging his shoulders complacently) : "I do not know. But what matters it? Two or three thousand, at the least."

E., opening up a fresh subject, speaks of Hayti as a nation.

Blue G. (aggressively): "France a republic, Hayti a republic, and America a republic"— (triumphantly shaking three fingers in E.'s face) — "three republics!"

E.: "You have been to Paris?"

Blue G. : "I will go next month. I will see the Exposition. I will review the troops."

(The Pink and Green Generals join in. To deepen the impression already made upon the Englishman they also, it seems, are going to Paris probably next month, and all three launch into a chaos of conversation.)

Blue G. (surviving the chorus): " Return here in two years' time, my friend. You will see changes. Railways will intersect the land. The army, already numerous, will be enormous. And I shall be again a Minister!"

As this seems to place a cap upon the future, the Englishman disengages himself from his companions and goes out into the stockade, where, beneath a tamarind tree, he finds his horse making frantic efforts to fight the puissant steed of the Pink General. He on-saddles and rides round by way of the piazza. The Pink General has fallen asleep open-mouthed, the voice of the Blue General rumbles on in continuous argument. He and the Green General are taking a friendly "Rhum" together. They call out their adieux as the Englishman passes, then a bend of the track shuts them out from his life for ever.

4

Vaudoux Worship and Sacrifice

Although much of the information incorporated in the following chapter was only gradually gained during the whole period of my stay in Hayti, I am giving it an early place in this volume, because some slight knowledge of what Vaudoux really is and its influence upon its votaries is indispensable to the understanding of the condition and character of the inhabitants of the Republic.

For Vaudoux is so inextricably woven in with every side of the Haytian's life, his politics, his religion, his outlook upon the world, his social and family relations, his prejudices and peculiarities that he cannot be judged apart from it.

The underpart of Black life is full of strange beliefs. In Hayti the nominal religion is Roman Catholicism, but it is no more than a thin veneer; beneath you find, not traces merely, but a solid groundwork of West African superstition, serpent-worship, and child-sacrifice.

This last assertion may seem almost incredible, made in connection with a nation, not only living in the midst of other civilised communities, but which was itself started a century ago on the double lines of European laws and a Christian creed. Nevertheless, all those who know anything of Hayti by personal experience and residence there, know too that the fact has been amply proved over and over again.

Little is known of the Black Republic outside of her own shores, and even at home her policy is a policy of keeping dark everything humiliating to her pretensions. The national method is not to suppress these infamous crimes, but simply to deny their existence.

The evil of Vaudoux worship is widespread. The Government has, at all times, been too unstable to care to take the risk of seriously opposing so powerful a combination. The sect is universally feared, hence they carry on their rites and their orgies with practical impunity.

At the root of this outgrowth of superstition are the Papalois and Mamalois, the priests and priestesses, who minister to the naturally credulous mind of the negro. Papaloi, Mamaloi, are corruptions of "Papa le roi" and "Mama le roi," the titles themselves showing the estimation in which these people are held. They dwell chiefly in the mountains. A famous priest lives on the road (save the mark!) between Port-au-Prince and Jacmel ; another towards Furcy; but the old iniquity who is more especially in my mind's eye sojourns in the sierras not so far from the capital itself.

Vaudoux, according to its more elect disciples, is an all-powerful deity, but the idea of the masses does not rise above the serpent, which represents to them their god and which presides, in its box, over all their services. These usually take place at night and in pseudo-secrecy. They consist of dancing, sacrificing, feasting, invocations, and a Delphic delirium on the part of the Mamaloi, winding up with scenes of an indescribable nature.

There are said to be two sects of Vaudoux ; one which sacrifices only fruits, white cocks, and white goats to the serpent-god ; the other, that sinister cult above referred to, whose lesser ceremonies call for the blood of a black goat, but whose advanced orgies cannot be fully carried out without the sacrifice of "the goat without horns" — the human child.

White is supposed to be the sacred colour of the former, red of the latter, but on one occasion I was lucky enough to witness a Vaudoux function where the flags and handkerchiefs were red and white, pointing to an intermingling of the two forms ; the cocks sacrificed were both black and white, again bearing evidence in the same direction.

Testimony as to the order of the ceremonies used in Vaudoux worship differs, but this is not be wondered at, being the natural result of an unwritten ritual, practised by an utterly ignorant people. Each writer on Hayti gives the order at secondhand as described by native witnesses, and probably all are equally right as regards the instance referred to.

For my own satisfaction I noted down on my cuff the sequence of the rites as they took place before me. Of these I will give a detailed description later.

The serpent used by these fetish sectaries is generally believed to be the Macajuel, a species allied to the harmless boa. When riding in a remote country district, I met a man with a snake of this kind that he had caught. I offered him five dollars for it, which he refused. The Haytian peasant is very poor, and five dollars is for him not merely a windfall, but absolute wealth, and he would hardly have declined it without strong reason for doing so.

Sir Richard Burton speaks of the "small green snake of the Haytian negroes, so well known by the abominable orgies enacted before the Vaudoux King and Queen." Today the green snake is extinct in the island. More than that, no white man I met would allow it ever existed, and I was almost beginning to think that Burton had for once made a mistake, when a certain old native, whom I may describe as up to the neck in Vaudoux, told me certain facts which modified my conclusion. I was subsequently shown a green snake preserved in spirits.

Whether the snake enclosed in its box on the Haytian altars of to-day during a child-sacrifice is of that species or a harmless boa it is impossible to say, as no white man has ever been allowed to set eyes upon one.

Vaudoux, Juju, Obi, or some analogous superstition seems to belong to the bottom stratum of black nature. Vaudoux is a religion of old, old time. When William the Norman came to England it was no doubt flourishing amongst the African tribes of the West Coast.

With the captured slaves, whose descendants the Haytians are, it was brought to this distant island, and here it is rampant still. It raises an unshamed head in all quarters. The last President was even said to be a votary. A large place like a casino, just outside of Port-au-Prince, is devoted to its observances.

But Southern Hayti is its strongest rallying-point, and Jacmel the hot-bed of its power. All along the road between the town and Port-au-Prince I know it thrives exceedingly. In the north, at Cap Haytien, on the contrary, the traces of it are slighter.

Vaudoux is cannibalism in the second stage. In the first instance a savage eats human flesh as an extreme form of triumph over an enemy; so the appetite grows until this food is preferred to any other. The next stage follows naturally. The man, wishing to propitiate his god, offers him that which he himself most prizes. Add to this sacrifice the mysteries and traditions of the ages, and you have the Vaudoux of to-day.

Cannibalism has been brought as a very general accusation against the Haytians, but although there is no doubt that the child sacrificed in the worst Vaudoux rites is afterwards dismembered, cooked, and eaten, I do not think that of recent years the practice of cannibalism, unconnected with sacrifice, is in any degree prevalent, although it is equally certain that scattered instances do still come to light. The Government have been known to make feeble and spasmodic efforts to punish the culprits, but as a rule this iniquity, as well as most others, is allowed to run its course unchecked.

To quote a case or two of these judicial attempts at punishment: — A woman and her daughter, convicted redhanded at Jacmel of killing and eating a child, were mounted on asses and beaten round the town by the police with cocomacaque clubs. Afterwards they were released. Two years ago, in the northern part of the island, a party of men and women were imprisoned for a few days only for the same crime, which they indulged in as a conclusion to a Vaudoux sacrifice. But this crime is, I both believe and hope, on the decrease and may in time die out.

Not the least prominent feature of Vaudoux is the drum that calls the worshippers together. One which I saw and examined was four feet high. Its frame was made of some jointed wood like bamboo, in girth it was as large as a man's trunk. The upper surface was of black goatskin, thinned by the thrumming of many fingers, with hair still adhering to the edges where it was pegged to the frame.

This instrument is so singularly constructed that although at a distance of a mile or more it sounds loudly, near at hand its throbbing note is indistinct and low.

Where the negro picked up this secret in acoustics it is hard to imagine. But the peculiarity has an important use. A sect with rites like the Vaudoux have naturally strong reasons for desiring that none but the initiated should be present at their gatherings : hence the low, misleading sound that mutters about you when the drum is played close at hand, whereas the initiated, who have warning of a sacrifice, hear the call at really wonderful distances, and at once proceed to the appointed spot.

The dificulty of following up the dull throb at close quarters is extraordinary. On several occasions I have tried to trace from the ear alone the unmistakable vibration, and have failed. There is some thrilling quality in the muffled and mysterious beat which cannot be described, but which stirs the pulse in spite of familiarity.

Hayti is the sole country with any pretence to civilisation where a superstition contaminated by such active horrors exists. It would seem that the perpetuation of a cult so degrading must have its source deep in the character of the race. Yet you find that these undoubted cannibals can on occasion be both kind-hearted and hospitable. Perhaps the root of all lies in their squalid ignorance.

Then whose is the fault?

The answer must be given unhesitatingly. It is the fault of the Government. Instead of rare and futile demonstrations directed against some outlying evildoer, they should strike at the Papalois, who are the heart and mainspring of Vaudouxism. Let them destroy the Papalois, and the whole edifice of horror will crumble to pieces of natural decay.

I made it a special point while in the island to learn as much of the sect as possible, to get at the truth concerning them by personal experience, and to glean actual facts at firsthand. With this object in view, I more than once gained intelligence of the time and place appointed for the performance of Vaudoux ceremonies and sacrifices. I wanted to see for myself the mysteries of snake-worship, and by good luck I succeeded to a certain extent.

On the first of these occasions, I understood that I must find my way to a low part of the town after night had fallen. It was getting on towards midnight when the muffled reverberation of a drum beating a swift measure came up out of the hot darkness ; no wind stirred, and the candle-flame by the open window stood up straight and unwavering.

I descended into the evil odours of the street. I had heard it before, that droning drum music, with a scream or two at intervals, which in Hayti often beats upon the overladen pulses of the night. The town was under martial law, but passing steps were stirring up the ineffable rubbish under foot. At the corner, "Qui vive." from a soldier in the gloom, but a small coin settled the matter and I passed on.

At last the challenges died away behind me ; the carpet of dirt and garbage seemed to have grown thicker below the tread : the streets were unlit even in the best quarters of the town, and therefore to keep clear of drains and arbitrary pools of slime was almost an impossibility.

Under a roof a concertina was playing to a crowd who oscillated and turned in dance measure, but the drum was calling from somewhere in the dark twist of streets beyond. Above shone the serene stars ; beneath them the negro and negress followed out their scheme of life. Past booths crowded with talkers, past the vending-places of rich, unwholesome sweetmeats and drink in coloured bottles, pausing occasionally to catch the vibration of the drum, across an open market-place frilled with an edging of empty sheds, and at length I was at the spot described to me.

There was a crowd round the house, peering through a window at the doings inside. A big negro stood at the door with a coco-macaque club. There was some demur as to admittance, then the door opened and a stream of muffled drum-music and a monotonous hum of voices broke out on the ear. A hand beckoned me, and I found myself within. The shutters were closed, and it was difficult through the obscurity to make out one's surroundings, but I felt the presence of a crowd. The song they were singing their forefathers sang two hundred years ago in the riverland of Africa.

Suddenly a negro set light to a candle, and at once the scene leapt out to meet the eye. The song ceased, but all mouths still hung upon its final note. There must have been upwards of two hundred people in two small rooms. They were ranged round the walls, those in front sitting on their haunches, leaving only a narrow passage open in the middle of the earthen floor. The faces were glistening with heat, and all eyes were turned towards the Mamaloi.

The silence was broken by an abrupt bark of the drum and the chant began again, the sitting figures swaying their shoulders to its roll. It was led by an enormous negress, wrapped in a white and purple print, who held a living cock in her spatulate black fingers—you could see the shining of her uncut nails. She sat and swayed and sang in what at last became an insistent drone of sound. It was like something heard through a delirium of fever, you could not forget or escape it for an instant, and the drum drove it through the brain with blows. It neither waxed nor waned ; it was merely the same, and endless.

Meantime the Mamaloi danced, back and forth, forth and back, between the knees of the worshippers. She was about forty years of age, small-faced, snub-nosed, roundeyed. She gazed past you with a rapt stare, a streak of foam lay across her chin. For covering she wore a thin white robe, tied with a red sash, and a string of gold beads gleamed round her neck. There were two candles alight now, set in pots and decked with the pink flowers of the melon. Beneath them, on the floor, was spread the feast; bottles of coloured intoxicants, Congo beans, ground rice, and red melon. At intervals the Mamaloi stopped to sprinkle water over them, and as she did so the song rose a little higher; but would it never end, never end? I had time to notice that the walls were ornamented with prints from the French illustrated papers. Upon how many strange scenes do those pictures look ! You find them everywhere in Hayti; in the drawing-rooms of the rich and in the huts of the peasantry, and now in a place used for Vaudoux rites.

The song rose suddenly in volume, a candle flickered and burnt up. Still the Mamaloi danced between the rows of knees with stealthy, menacing, tigerish steps. Her excitement was intensifying, her eyes seemed to grow larger, but they never met yours. As she danced she cleared her throat and spat with a noise like artillery coming into action. The huge black woman in the centre droned on, and to the drum-beat was added the chink of a key on metal. The Mamaloi quickened in her sinuous dancing. The heat was terrific ; humanity sweltered there. And over all presided a portrait of the German Emperor, whose eye I seemed to catch at this juncture.

The Papaloi, a small and filthy old man, crouched at one side, as the Mamaloi caught the cock from the hands of the big woman, and, holding it by the neck, flung it over her head and shoulder. Her face was distorted with frenzy ; round and round she twisted, accompanied by a swifter measure of the same ciead song. She laid the cock upon the heads of the worshippers and began to whirl more and more rapidly to the hurrying, maddening drumming. Suddenly she straightened her arm, spun the cock round and round, its flapping wings beating impotently upon the air. A snowstorm of feathers floated up as she stood with rapt eyes and bared teeth, twirling; then she flung up her hand, and the headless body flew over her shoulder.

Her excitement was horrible ; she pressed the bleeding neck to her lips, and, when she slowly withdrew her hand, stood for an instant fixed and immovable, her lips and teeth stained red. Then she began to run up and down screaming; at last she staggered and fell, and, with the torn neck of the sacrifice still in her hand, rolled in under the feet of the worshippers, while the song boiled over her.

In the interval various fetishes were brought out of a box, uncouth wooden images, stones and bones, old and overhandled, which must have come over with the ancestors of these people from their original home.

After this the rites, dancing, sacrifice, sprinkling of blood and of some pungent fluid, which was certainly not perfume, followed one another in changing order. Six cocks were slain, all in like manner to the first, with like monotony and brutishness. One of them, however, was the chief sacrifice, and its blood was set apart in a basin by itself. With this blood the Mamaloi went outside and sprinkled the doors and gates, putting marks upon them.

Then she returned, and with the remainder sealed the foreheads of those present with the sign of the Cross !

This intermingling of the ancient Jewish and Christian symbolisms with their own nauseous ceremonies springs, of course, from their acquaintance with Roman Catholic teaching. The ignorant are always ready to incorporate the worship of any other god with their own : from their point of view it can do no harm, and may do some good.

After a time the frenzy grew, and the dancing became universal. The whole crowd were moving and swaying and jostling together, chattering out the unvarying, monotonous measure. The chink of the old key quickened riotously, the drum thrummed out under the falling thumb-joints with stimulating haste, the mental atmosphere fermented and rose to high pressure. They swung and whirled, they writhed and danced in an intoxication of excitement.

A woman was contorting herself and hissing in an ill-lighted corner. Near the end of the room another with a child at her breast was carried away by the seething hysteria about her, and began to shuffle to and fro, with eyes distended in a sort of sightless stare. There was hardly room for all, and the drums beat faster. The child at the breast began to stretch its arms and wail, but the mother danced blindly on.

Still the tumult and the music grew. The atmosphere was suffocating, but there was no symptom of tiring or cessation. On and on and on, the scene with its savagery and blood and senselessness sickened you. When at last I got out into the clear starshine once more I felt I could not have endured another five minutes of it. Yet what I had witnessed was only the beginning of an orgie which was to go on for a couple of days longer.

The belief of a people is the skeleton on which its character is moulded. Here in Hayti they have this gigantic cult, superstition, call it what you will, possessing unbounded influence, and in active existence, as I have personally seen, all over the island. The tremendous hold it has gained over the people is proved by the fact, well known and amply verified on many an occasion, that a mother will, under the orders of the Papaloi, give up her own offspring to be sacrificed. When reproached with inhumanity, the reply has more than once been given: "Who had a better right to eat them than I who brought them forth?"

No picture of Hayti will remain longer in my memory than the remembrance of a mean old man in grass slippers, heel-less, showing a long half-foot of veiny black ankle under the faded trouser, the upper half of him almost bare, the whole topped by a vinegar-coloured face graven by time and wickedness into exaggerated wrinklings. He had wideopen, far-away eyes, and sparse grey hair scattered on chin and lip and head.

He was a Papaloi, or Vaudoux priest, otherwise a Haytian witch-doctor and medicine-man. His home was far away up in the mountains, where he dwelt as a patriarch. He owned four palm-thatched huts within an enclosure of raw stakes, where, hidden away among the potato-green foliage of the bush, tamarinds, bananas, and mangoes ripened. All day long he sat in the shade, and his wives waited upon him. There were four of them, and their ages ranged from sixty to sixteen. He was said to have other wives elsewhere, but, then, he could afford it, for he was a man of substance, and his fame was great in the land.

In Hayti the Papaloi is a living force. He is at once a high priest and a consulting physician. He will cure the body, and, for a consideration, touch the hidden springs of life. People are very much afraid of him. They travel up on foot, on donkey-back and pony-back, according to their stations in life, from the plains to consult him; and, for payment, he will use his hereditary knowledge on their behalf. He can cure, and he can kill, and the two are often curiously allied in his practice.

A man has a revenge to accomplish; he seeks a Papaloi. He is the victim of an unrequited affection, he seeks the Papaloi. He is sick, he seeks the Papaloi. The Papaloi is, in fact, the pivot on which moves much of Haytian life. All these powers over mind and body he lays claim to, and in the matter of love some of his cures are nasty enough, but there is one thing he can assuredly do — he can give you a revenge for twenty dollars that would satisfy the vindictiveness of a Corsican and leave him a balance of remorse. The Papaloi can take away your reason, with or without pain, at will. His ancient subtleties of poisoning are unapproached. Of course, he winds into his woof much useless mystery and ceremony of time and place and circumstance. This is natural, as well as useful and politic, for a mere dose would seem of poor value to a sickness-smitten negro compared with a remedy to be swallowed when the moon is at her full, with mystic rites and incantations and the bones of the dead thrown in.

Nor is the white man outside the powers of the Papaloi. Consider the simplicity of being poisoned. You unwittingly offend a negro and he takes away with him the sense of deadly injury. You eat and drink three times a day, and on one occasion or another he seizes his chance, and puts the Papaloi's prescription into your food or drink. Then sickness grips you, ghastly sickness, and you are far beyond the aid of doctors of your own colour. Some poison, old as the world, is at your vitals. You must infallibly seek a Papaloi or die. Being the local practitioner, he may be the very man who has poisoned you. For twenty dollars, or perhaps for as many centimes, he has brought this evil upon you, and he asks a liberal advance on the first sum to cure you. It is a mere matter of antidote. No man but shudders at the grasp of these grim powers, they are so potent and so hopelessly irresistible. You pay the Papaloi fifty dollars ; you would pay him a thousand as readily for no more than the feeling of relief.

To his credit be it said, he usually keeps his side of the contract ; though he occasionally uses delay to extort a little more. The real wonder of it is that he does not spread his poisons broadcast, but it would appear that he uses his power not for play, but for pay, or to carry out some personal resentment. Once an attempt of this kind was made under my own close observation,— a little something in a little water-and-rum, — but it came to no serious issue.

During my travels in the interior I carried a waterbottle of military pattern topped by a cup of black vulcanite, which was padlocked securely over the neck. In this I usually carried some Haytian rum and water. On one occasion I left the bottle at a hut, where I had bought corn for my horse, while I went down to the river to bathe. On my return I started with my guide and a pair of villagers. After a time it occurred to me that a drink all round would be acceptable. I offered it. To my surprise it was somewhat furtively refused. My suspicions were aroused, and I also went thirsty. I afterwards discovered that some vegetable poison had been put into the bottle ; the leathern strap padlocked over the cup had been stretched, the cup turned, and the poison inserted. I could not imagine any reason for the attempt. It seemed quite gratuitous. Not till long after did a possible solution flash upon me. I had petted a little plump child at the hut, which, I believe, is in certain cases considered unlucky. Perhaps they thought I had the evil eye. Certainly, as the Zulus say, my snake stood up beside me that day. I do not care to think over the incident, for Haytian poisons do not kill painlessly, and I was alone in the heart of the mountainous interior, miles away from a white face.

In a word, secret poisoning pervades the scheme of Haytian life exactly as it pervades that of West Africa.

There was an English engineer at Petit Goave — he has now left Hayti, so I am free to tell the story — who discharged a workman for a serious fault, and shortly after left the place for Port-au-Prince. Arrived in the capital, his legs began to swell with all the symptoms of the wellknown African disease beri-beri. He consulted doctors, but they could do nothing for him. Making a pretty accurate guess at the true state of the case, he at length sent a messenger to the Papaloi at Petit Goave.

The Papaloi demanded fifty dollars, and promised for that sum to effect a certain cure. The Englishman agreed to pay, and the Papaloi, with many incantations, prepared a bath of leaves, a thick brown bath. Into this the sick man was plunged, and after three days was well enough to return to Petit Goave. But the beri-beri returned, and he was obliged to consult the Papaloi once more, who said that he had again been poisoned, and that for a second payment of fifty dollars he would again cure him, at the same time warning him that if he were poisoned a third time he would probably die. The white man took the hint, and, as soon as he was cured, left the country.

The Papaloi is descended straight from the African witchdoctor. Seven generations ago he was a secret king among the slaves of French Hayti ; further back still he lived in a wattle hut by the Congo and made Juju. And he makes it in Hayti to this day. Here and there in talk with him you stumble across some older African superstition, something from which you could, without other evidence, deduce the origin of his race.

There is another operation to which the Papalois — or more often the Mamalois — turn their power. They can produce a sleep which is death's twin brother. For instance, a child marked for the Vaudoux sacrifice is given a certain drug, shivers and in some hours sinks into a stillness beyond the stillness of sleep. It is buried in due course, and later, by the orders of the Papalois, is dug up and brought to consciousness; of what occurs then I have written in another place. It is ghoulish and horrible, but beyond all question human sacrifice is offered up to a considerable extent in the Black Republic at the present time.

Everywhere in Hayti you find charms against evil, sold by Papalois and Mamalois. They assume all shapes — sticks, stones, rags, and bags of leaves. I remember seeing a 'bus, as they call the local cab, overturn in Port-auPrince. The first thing that the driver scrambled for was a nameless bundle which had fallen from under the seat. It was his charm against being upset!

Putting Vaudoux upon their enemies is another variation of the priests' accomplishments. A bundle of garbage is placed at your door, and if you pass over it you are sure, the negroes say, to fall ill. So far the thing is absurd, but it becomes less so when the action of the rotten egg on our doorstep is aided by a sprinkling of powdered glass in your rice. No priestcraft gains so firm a grip of the savage mind as that which lends solid temporal aid to the passions of its devotees. There is a deep desire ingrained in the black to get a pinch on the man above him ; to be given this obscurely and surely is sufficient to rivet his adhesion to any faith. Few whites in the island have altogether escaped the far-off touch of the Papaloi directed against them for some inscrutable offence by those who are most probably of their own household.

In considering the character and influence of the Papaloi, one fact should be borne in mind ; that he is the sacrificial priest when the most culpable and hideous of the Vaudoux rites is practised. He is also the guiding and dominant intelligence amongst the bulk of his countrymen, the result of which must be a continuous falling back deeper and deeper into the savage state. But as long as Hayti retains an entirely negro Government, at least so long will the shadow of the Papaloi loom large in the land, for Africa transplanted is Africa still, and she is so conservative that the passage of uncounted years finds her ever the same.

The Papaloi is the rain-maker, the witch-doctor of West Africa under another name. He is a kind of fortunate vagabond battening upon the ignorance and credulity of this New World negro. He is dirtier than an Indian fakir, without that excuse which emanates from the religion of the fakir, to whose mind our precept assumes an inverted form — with him dirtiness is next to godliness. But the Papaloi, on the other hand, has no religion in his dirt; he is filthy, because to be clean is troublesome. And the Papaloi possesses a treble share of the universal laziness of the children of Ham.

Rut he is not a subject to jest at. His power is paramount throughout the length and breadth of the Republic; he rules with an iron hand, and with that jealous insidious grasp on the whole inner life of his fellow-countrymen which is everywhere the distinctive trait of priestcraft. From the highest to the lowest all yield him obedience; it is true the majority believe, but the minority, who do not believe, at least tremble. The whole land is netted over with fear, fear of vague and occult potencies that harass and harm and hurt, and in case of revolt inevitably kill.

Remove the Papaloi and the murders and superstitious observances would, to a large extent, die out, and the land shake off the influence which keeps it so degraded. The debasing consequences of kindred superstitions acting on the negro mind is keenly recognised in other countries where the black man does not rule himself. Among the American negroes the rites of Voodoo, Voudoo,

Vaudoo, Vaudoux — you can spell it as you like — are carried on in secrecy, and sedulously screened from light of day.

In Jamaica the punishment for the practice of Obeah is imprisonment and whipping, the latter having a wholesomely deterrent effect. For, though Obeah is to its Haytian variant as water is to wine, the danger of it lies in the fact that if unchecked it would only too easily merge into the enormities and crimes which distinguish true Vaudoux worship. Obeah is a cult of charm-wearing, of love-potions, of the laying on of curses by means more or less absurd, such as the tying of a bunch of red rags to a branch near your door, or hanging up a beer bottle filled with nasty concoctions, all of which go to prove its kinship in a puny degree with the hideous Haytian sect.

It must be remembered that it is the Papaloi who is the instigator and upholder of the vilest forms of snake-worship, and they can be carried on by him with practical impunity. When some grosser case than usual forces itself upon the public notice it is never the priest who suffers. The victim is always some obscure votary, never the arch-criminal, who is too powerful for the Government to interfere with. A couple of unknown women, or a group of poverty-stricken peasants, will be maltreated or imprisoned, or even on occasion shot, while the Papaloi is permitted to go scot-free.

If you are a black man, either you belong to the sect and are under deadly compulsion to perform the behests of the Papaloi, or else you are not of the sect, and, as its supposed enemy, are exposed to equally deadly dangers. It is thus very evident that in a land publicly christened with the names of Liberty and Brotherhood no man is free.

The mysterious weapon of poison — which can kill body, or mind, or both, or merely cause long languishing and pain — is one against which no man can at all times guard himself. And this is the chief weapon the Papaloi, with his pre-eminent knowledge of vegetable venoms, is apt to use.

To give yet another illustration. I knew a negro in the Triburon peninsula who was not of the sect of the Vaudoux. He was at one time a white man's servant; he stood between his master and harm, and he was not to be bribed. Nor did he buy charms to wear round his neck or inside his shirt. Hence it was prophesied tiiat he would not remain long in the employment he then held. He never knew where he drank it for certain, but drink it he did, — a malignant drug. It had its effects swiftly. He rolled in the gutters. He stared at the sun with vacant eyes — to use his own expressive words: "My head was filled with boiling blood." His master noticed his condition, and sent him to a white doctor, who gave him civilised medicines, which had no effect whatever. At last he was taken to a Papaloi in the mountains, who gave him a compost of drugs in an earthen jug. He ate of it, and was cured. He had paid his tax to the powers of darkness and of the soil.

Even in the highest places the hand of the Papaloi makes itself felt. Since it is a matter of public notoriety that he can kill his enemy in a number of painful ways, none dare offend him. He is a licensed criminal.

Occasionally he will admit to the white man that he is a bit of a fraud, but for the most part he keeps up appearances. How much he believes in his own pretensions or in Vaudoux as a religion it is im-possible to guess. He uses both to forward his own ends. He seldom has a tendency towards discussion. His argument in favour of the sacred snake is old as the hills. "You have an enemy," he says, "who is not a snake-worshipper. I will put Vaudoux upon him. If his god be stronger than mine, he will save him." Afterwards poison is con-veyed into the victim's food, and when the man dies the Papaloi's disciples agree that the serpent is a great god indeed.

The Papalois feed like leeches upon their negro following. The country is honey-combed by that system of terrorism. The profession is not necessarily hereditary, although the son often follows in the footsteps of his father. The knowledge of poisons, which is, after all, their stock-intrade, passes down through the generations, nor will they, any more than the Indian jugglers, divulge any particle of their secret lore. These priests are no doubt to a certain extent hypnotists. They achieve the unexplainable. And, of course, what is to us a trick is to the savage mind a miracle.

In full dress a Papaloi makes at once a grotesque and an alarming figure. His piecemeal vestments are red, the sacred colour; his aged face, bandaged about the brows with a red handkerchief, peers out malignantly. It is he who in the course of the ceremonies initiates the hysteric fervour and delirium of the priestess and the worshipping crowd; it is he again who leads the orgies into frenzied and horrible excesses which it is impossible to describe. These orgies continue for three or four days at a time, and their result must infallibly lead to the continuous debasement of the national character.

There is no doubt also that the priests prompt the action of the 'Toup-garous", the child-stealers, who are usually women, generally old, pilot-fishes to the priestly sharks. The Papaloi chooses the victim, but it is the " loup-garou " who steals it or otherwise secures it. The drugged child is borne away to some secure place, be it a hut in the centre of a town or in some lonely forest clearing. The little body bears all the appearance of death, and so it is allowed to remain until the appointed time, when an antidote to the sleeping drug is given, and the dazed child wakes to become the central figure in a tragedy of sacrifice.

What are the three galls of this priest-ridden people?

First, there is superstition. Who keeps it alive?

Next, there are the impure and tragical rites. Who instigates them ?

Lastly, there is the opposition to all enlightenment. Who obscures the light?

In every case the answer is the same. The Papalois.

Their own manner of life, their traditions, their very appearance, their budget of endeavours are all mean, self-seeking, squalid. They have absolutely no good point, no clean impulse; no characteristic that you can even distantly respect.

It is well to understand exactly the position these men occupy in Hayti. In the unhealthy atmosphere which they create evil becomes alive and flourishes. They encourage the worst tendencies innate in negro nature as assiduously as a gardener nourishes his forcing-beds. They permeate Hayti with their influence. Until they are smitten down the country can never flourish.

At present the greatest obstacle to an almost universal terrorism is the sprinkling of white men dwelling in the coast towns. The better Haytians are ashamed of Vaudoux, but they are afraid of its revenge. The Government are either unwilling or unable to cope with it. In West Africa the first endeavour of the advancing white is to break the rule of the witch-doctors, and they succeed in so far that superstition moves slowly backwards into the heart of Africa. But in Hayti, instead of meeting with relentless opposition the Papaloi meets with tacit encouragement, or at best a puerile interference, with results such as I have even now only partially shown. As the case stands, were one to subtract the very small white element, his authority would increase fourfold. And it is in the mountainous interior, where no white man goes, that his autocracy reaches its high water mark.

But it is absurd to pretend that the Papaloi possesses supernatural powers, though I would not deny for a moment that he has inherited certain knowledge which seems at present to lie outside the white man's range. He is a Borgia in poisons, and to fill in the rest of his hollow pretensions he is an actor, a colossal quack, and a terrorist.

5

The Haytian Navy

Most nations keep a navy to fight against their foes. In this extraordinary country the navy couples that mission with the high honour of being a potential factor towards either internal peace or war. The case stands thus. Hayti is a place somewhat given over to political strife; a country in which, as has been said of Mexico, "all things are possible, and most things come to pass," a country in which an enterprising man can easily bring off a coup d'etat.

For the last eleven years there has been no bloody revolution such as the past has so often seen, but there have been two or three attempts to upset the Government, and under Hippolyte a good deal of quiet shooting. Portau-Prince might quite conceivably go to sleep under one Government, and wake up under another. But to-day the capture of the Capital would only be equivalent to carrying the entrenchments of a fort — the inner bastions would still remain, and the navy answers to the bastions.

You may see it every day at anchor in the harbour, four ships in a line. One presented a sufficiently ghastly aspect, its tubby white sides being splashed and smeared with red paint in a manner horribly suggestive of human blood. This was the " Dessahnes ", and as she remained in the same unsightly condition during the whole period of my stay in Port-au-Prince I incline to believe that the Haytian Navy had run out of paint.

But the show ship is the "Crete-a-Pierrot", the third in the line that runs across from the lighthouse to the Bizoton side of the bay. She is a fat, white vessel with a yellow funnel and gold scroll-work upon her bows and stern, and over her floats the angry blue and red of the Black Republic. Away on the lighthouse side is the "Toussaint", a cargo steamer of chequered career; once a fruit boat, next a Haytian warship, now a sad example of the pilfering habits of the personnel of the navy. In the words of the bull-necked, slouch-hatted mate of an American sailing ship : "They're a set of thieves. You wouldn't believe, but I've had niggers off that ship come here with brasswork they've scofted. Yes, and boiler-fittings — anything, any blooming thing for which they thought they'd get a red cent. Why, I know a captain in this trade who was offered fittings that must have cost this chirruping black Government thousands of dollars, for any bid he liked to make. Jes' you go and see I"

And so it was. A few boys lived hugger-mugger in the stripped, deserted hulk, the tides beat a tattoo on her rotten skin, and she was full of rats and empty noises.

Then, having seen the worst of the Haytian Navy, I decided to go and see the best of it. Therefore upon a certain December morning an ancient rowboat, propelled by the united exertions of two small negroes, crawled slowly out upon the lazy blue waters of Port-au-Prince Bay.

"*Blanc,* which sheep you go for?"

"There's an Englishman in command of one. Put me on board of her."

The pink conch-shells, the sucking fish, and the lump of white coral loaded down the old leaky boat. At some risk of up-setting it was pulley-hauled out towards the centre of the bay where the " Crete-a-Pierrot " lay blistering under a scalding sun. She was designed at the request of the Haytian Government in England. The plans in due time were forwarded to Hayti, where one Minister took upon himself to move the ward-room a few yards forward, and another thought the engine-room might with great profit to the Republic be shifted a few feet to starboard. When they had had their will of them, the revised plans were sent back to the designer, who, so the story goes,

said that either he or the Haytian Government must design the ship. In the event they thought it well to leave it to him. So the end of it was that the " Crete-a-Pierrot " was finished, built in England, armed in France, and three years ago was added to the Haytian Navy.

"Blanc," said the small negro, "the Anglais is leaving the sheep." And through the dancing heat-haze I saw a white gig being manned ; a figure descended the gangway, the squeak of rowlocks followed, and the boat slipped out from the warship's shadow.

With a gasp and a gurgle my boat gathered more way. I had not braved the sun and the unsavoury approaches to the wharves for nothing, and another opportunity of catching the English com-mander might not readily present itself. The warship's gig came on with laborious strokes. and when within hailing distance :

"May I go and take a look over your ship, sir?"

"Hey, what's that.' Got a pass from the admiral?"

"Afraid I haven't."

"They won't let you aboard without."

"Thanks, sorry to have troubled you."

There was a silence. Then Captain Gilmour drew out his watch.

"I've a few minutes to spare. I'll come back and show you over."

It took some moments to get my boat alongside the gangway. Rarely has a foreign navy been visited in so unimposing a craft.

THE WHARF AT PORT-AU-PRINCE.

Captain Gilmour, R. N. R., is a Scotsman who served in the Ashanti business, and is now under contract with the Haytian Government to command their best warship. He is a sunburnt, kindly man, who takes a very real interest in his work.

"You are heavily armed," I said, looking round.

"Why, yes. Gunner!" A grinning black stepped forward and opened the breech of a big gun. It shone clean and oily. "We are pretty heavily armed, as you say. For'ard there we carry a sixteen centimetre gun. This is a twelve, and there are four tens besides. Also we have five Nordenfeldts, two five-barrelled, the others three. Those, with two inch and a half Maxims, are all the ironmongery we carry."

The guns were clean and in excellent order, and the decks bore evidence of recent stoning, but Captain Gilmour told me that had I come a week later things would have been still more shipshape.

"She steams fifteen knots and carries a crew of one hundred and seventy-five. My chief engineer is a white man, and my first lieutenant a Barbadian, who was formerly in the merchant service. Yes, the admiral comes aboard sometimes. Admiral Killick. A Haytian? Yes. He used to command a barque. I brought this ship out from England, and my chief engineer came with me. I am under contract with the Government here for three years more. Do I like it.? Oh, yes. If you'll step this way I'll show you the accommodation."

"Do you do much target practice."" I asked.

"Well, no, not with the big guns. But we do what we can. We tie a rifle on them and shoot with it up to 1,000 or 1,500 yards. It teaches the men to work the gun, you know, and is nearly as good as the real thing, besides being less expensive."

"Have you taken her any long cruises?" I said as he ushered me into the cabin, where a portrait of the president looked down upon the scene.

" We don't go farther than Jacmel and the Cape. Named after? After a battle when the I laytians drove the French out of the island. Well, I don't think there's any more to see. She'd have been more shipshape next week. I'll give you a cast ashore in my boat if you care for it."

As we left the ship, and the six negro rowers settled down into their slow, jerky stroke, I said:

"Do you think that if the occasion arose your men would — er — rise to it?"

Captain Gilmour stroked his chin.

"I do," he said. " When there was that German trouble here in December '97, they sent two warships, as you know, to try and force an indemnity out of this country.

Well, we were cleared for action, the men lying down behind their guns, and I have never in all my life seen so grim a look of determination on any faces as I saw then on theirs. Yes, I think they'd put up a very good fight indeed."

"You get a fair class of men then?"

"We do. The pay's good, though they don't always get it quite to time. The Government has embarrassments, you know."

We were nearing the wharf, and each stroke of the oars raised mud and smell.

"You don't lose men from yellow fever or that sort of thing?"

" No, we hardly ever have a case of sickness. These fellows are mostly immune, anyway."

Captain Gilmour gave an order in Creole.

"I don't speak it," he explained, "or French either. But I can give my orders in both. Many of my men can speak English. The authorities chose them with a view to that when I first came out."

The boat paddled along, looking among the rotten, black, and jagged piles for a landing-place.

"In that German business," said Captain Gilmour reminiscently, as the boathook caught, " we should have sunk the 'Charlotte' for certain. She was right under our guns. Be careful of that plank. It's loose. No, you won't take a cocktail? Well, good-bye."

6

Across Hayti

I HAD lingered so long in the city that the prospect of leaving its fetid streets behind me to breathe the purer air beyond their influence was very welcome. On my way to San Domingo I rode out of the capital towards the Plain of Cul-de-Sac, which in the days of the French occupation had contained many flourishing plantations, the soil being rich and productive beyond the average even in prolific Hayti.

"Yes, sir, you are right plumb in the centre of the most fertile district in Hayti — in the world. Do you know how much the revenue from this Plain of Cul-de-Sac totted up to in the time of the French colony a hundred years back? It was 20,000,000 francs, and what would you put it at now.'"

I had overtaken the speaker. I looked round. We were riding up a steady but hardly perceptible incline, and were in the heart of the plain. Ever since the first streak of dawn I had been passing ruined walls matted with vegetation, a few irregular patches of corn, a few clumps of Guinea grass about each solitary palm-thatched hut, yet mangoes, bananas, and tamarinds bore witness to the soil's unaided fruitfulness. As we went on the surroundings grew more lonely. Save for the town of Pompadette no village broke the desolate ranges of forest on either hand.

Here among wild and hardy trees some hint of the old-time occupation of man might be traced in the existence of gentler-bred shrubs, but the splendid country houses of the French period had apparently been absorbed by the jungle, which had closed in about them when man ceased to dwell there. Mules, bred between the parrot and the blackbird, chattered in the riotous foliage, and droves of lean pigs eked out a precarious existence on the land that the forest had reclaimed from the dominion of man.

"The present revenue? I have not an idea," I replied.

My questioner laughed. "Not a red cent, sir! Each year the forest comes forward, and no effort is made to keep the ground clear, much less to cultivate it. There is a proverb in this island which you may have heard — 'In Hayti there are only three classes who work; the white man, the black woman, and the ass.' What would it cost to lay a railroad along? Just nothing. And a rail would tap the plain and the lakes. Sir, if America owned this country there would be a track here before midsummer. As it is, the place is dead and getting deader. It tires me to look at it."

The Plain of Cul-de-Sac is, roughly, twenty-seven miles by twenty- four. Port-au-Prince lies at one end of it, and there the ships of all nations offer a ready outlet to its wealth. And yet, for all practical purposes, its wealth is not. A few huts, primitive enough to cost the labour of but half a day, lie scattered over its surface, but the occupiers are satisfied to subsist on the produce of the land as Nature gives it into their hands. The very sugar-boiling pans of a hundred years ago lie rusting where the dawn of slave-emancipation found them, and in these evidences of a bygone prosperity the lizard has its dwelling-place.

STREET SCENE IN PETIT GOÂVE.

Yet the people are poor, sordidly poor. They eke out a living, as the pigs do, upon the wild fruits they are too lazy and too improvident to cultivate. They glean wherewith to exist from that which French energy bequeathed to them. The wild descendants of the coffee shrubs planted by the settlers still bear berries, which the negroes are almost too idle to pick; and if there is a rainy season of unusual duration they pick them green. As for cleaning or caring for the shrubs, such a thing is never thought of save in isolated cases.

The negroes lounge away their lives in the sun, reckoning their age by the Presidents who come and go in the town by the sea. Nature does all their thinking for them, provides them with necessaries, the sole article she fails to supply them with being clothes, and they are rapidly coming to think clothes a superfluity. All that savours of civilisation is a legacy of the white nations who sent their battalions to win a colony which eventually slipped through the fingers of them all.

England gave Hayti the road I was traversing. It has degenerated into a bridle-path, but the great frame of it can still be discerned, clear and straight, and eloquent of the strong arm which cut it out from the virgin forest. But a hundred years of utter neglect has ruined it. It is perhaps sixty feet wide, in many places wider, but it is so maimed and damaged that only a slender line beaten down by the passing feet of asses is passable.

The interior of the huts by the wayside showed stark and bare; a cobbled floor was a sign of enterprise, but for the most part the earth, hardened by the feet of the inmates, did duty for the house-floor. Stars looked in through many a palm thatch. For the rest, a mat to sleep upon, gourds to hold water, a cooking pot, a couple of game-cocks tethered in a corner, with a broken chair or two, formed all their belongings, while flat-sided pigs fought with hens and guinea-fowls for any chance refuse of food.

Once a week most of the adults and all the children, make for the nearest market to barter Guinea-grass for tafia, what they have for what they have not.

Passing through this dreamlike land you often heard the noise of drums, or you came in sight of a single individual dancing alone in a clearing. It was a happy existence, no doubt, where the future was always left to adju.st itself.

At length the mountain-bordered plain gave way to swamp, high green tufts of Guinea-grass standing in pools of black water. I crossed a river some half an hour before I came in sight of the village of Thomazeau. It was merely an African collection of huts lumped in clusters, each cluster within its own stockade, with scant vestige of plant or tree about them. The red-shot sunset had given way to a pale green overhead and purple tropic dusk below. I was very hungry as I rode through the open part of the village, which was merely a space of bare earth.

On inquiry it turned out that the man in whose hut I had intended to pass the night had left early that morning for a neighbouring hamlet, and was not expected to return till the next day. This was sad, but food seemed the first and most urgent necessity ; the problem of finding a place to sleep in could be faced later on.

Ambling slowly on, I asked a likely-looking woman where, if anywhere, I might hope to get something to eat. She said she did not know, but, as an after-thought, suggested that there was a cock-fight going on at the other end of the village, and that *le blanc* might as well try there.

The cock-fight was taking place inside one of the usual enclosures, under the shelter of a wall-less roof, which rose above the scene on its corner posts like a four-stemmed brown toadstool. It was a manifestly critical moment in the cockpit, for three tiers of gesticulating negroes were bending over it with craning necks, raving in their excitement. My arrival was almost unnoticed, so I reined up to wait until public interest had simmered down.

In two or three minutes a long-drawn exclamation arose from the crowd, a white bird, splashed with ominous red, was gathered up by an angry-looking negro, and you could hear the victor crowing joyfully in the ring. Upon this the women with the baskets of bottles containing red and yellow drinks left the outskirts of the crowd to squat beneath the palisade.

To one of these I addressed myself. Could I get a fowl? No. A turkey.' No; nothing save pork. Rut I had too intimate a knowledge of the habits of Haytian pork in the pig stage to find the offer alluring, even though I had been in the saddle since daylight. In the long run I succeeded in securing "biscuits" of sour bread and a few brown, seed-covered, gluey cakes, with which I went off to seek for a lodging. As I passed up the street for the second time, a Haytian with a grey beard and a well-cut mouth came towards me.

"Do you sleep to-night at Thomazeau?" he asked civilly, and on my saying yes, he placed his house at my disposal.

This courteous old gentleman turned out to be the magistrate of the village. The ancient virtue of hospitality still flourishes in the rural districts ; it is a very marked characteristic in Hayti, and is absolutely disinterested, for the offer of payment mortally offends. My host took charge of my horse, sent off a small boy to cut a bundle of grass, to which I added corn, and then ushered me into his hut. He introduced me to his wife, an old lady in blue print, who brought me a cane-backed chair and busied herself in laying out my purchases on a table cloth.

When I had finished my meal, my host led me across the stockade to a hut where a mattress was spread on the floor, and there, with the help of my flask and a cigar, we passed the hour that is ended all over the island by the bugle call. We had discussed the possibilities of tobacco-culture, for he had brought me some native tobacco, and talked of the birds that haunt the lakes and one or two other subjects when the bugle sounded.

Just across the road was the local guard-house. In front of it the soldiers paraded, seven of them, under the General de la Place, or Governor, and finally disappeared into their hut. My host bade me good-night. I blew out the oil lamp, but then the mosquitoes, and with them hordes of sand-flies, came out to hold revel in the gloom. The last thing I remembered was a firefly with its pale lamp of intermittent green lighting up the dark roof.

In the morning, between night and dawn, I parted from my friend the magistrate and rode to the limit of the plain where the mountains began to swell upwards and a breakneck track led away over the round backs of the lower hills. They were green and heavily forested, and amongst them bird-life became noticeably more abundant.

Dawn grew to day, and day to afternoon ; the road commended itself to attention as one of the worst even in Hayti. Almost perpendicular in places, peppered with loose sliding falls of stone, overhung by branches and intertwining creepers — if the ingenuity of man ever constructed a highway here it had vanished out of all recognition. On and up, with a peep at some towering summit or flowing outline of a blue, far-off ridge, and hour by hour the forest closed in behind, shutting one off from the life of the ordinary world.

Soon I learned to expect one prominent feature wherever a clearing in the trees showed the presence of man. Whatever owed its origin to human handiwork was falling into decay and ruin, while Nature, fresh and vigorous, was always advancing her out-posts to the verge of each little circle and plot where the frail ragged dwellings held their own, like forlorn hopes that might at any time be ruthlessly smothered in the living tide of rank foliage.

So I went on, lingering by the way, eating the food I obtained from the negroes and sleeping beside their huts. One day was very like another. The people in the lonely groups of hovels only seemed to grow more poor, more ignorant, more superstitious, and in some ways more degraded as I penetrated further into the interior of the country. Few had enterprise enough to go to any place more distant than the nearest market, everyone lived from hand to mouth and seemed content to have it so.

Native life showed few attractions, no new features presented themselves, even individuality appeared to die out in that stagnation of existence.

One evening I was seated on a mat of water-reeds in the shadow of an old hut, the single room of which gave shelter night by night to eleven natives.

Compared to this, Thomazeau was civilisation incarnate.

The scene before me consisted of a few isolated huts huddled together inside a dilapidated stockade. Old Papa, the patriarch of this disparate knot of human beings, sat in shadow, dozing on a broken-down bench. In the foreground, under the usual four-legged toadstool roof, a fire smouldered, about which two or three girls were squatting, and the smoke curled lazily out into the sunlight. A youth, clothed only in a torn coat, which he used as a loin-cloth, was gnawing at a banana in the middle distance. Beside these, nothing but tamarinds, sand-flies, sun, and dust.

Papa was a senile figure, with a wrinkled mild old face. For thirty years he had watched the slow decay of things and of himself. I warmed him into life with a little rum, and he chattered innocuously of times forgotten, when Boyer was President and he, the old fossil, was young.

He had seen strong men shot down and buried, whose very graves have been lost for half a century, for Boyer was in power in the twenties. He was, undoubtedly, "old, old," as he called himself, and his wife was old, old, also, and so was everything that was his. His children and grandchildren were dead. The fourth generation lived around him, and his grandson's grandson brought fire to light his pipe.

All around the stockade the trees bore witness to the mischievous spirit of the dwellers there. The machette, a knife like a cutlass, had been used for wanton destruction often, sometimes to extract gum; in all cases the trees so wounded were dying. These people were the poorest I had come across; they might have almost belonged to a lower race.

They were dirty and squalid beyond imagination, some went naked. A bow-legged boy, long-armed as a gorilla, evidently half-witted, prowled about making beast noises, or shambled with an attempt at the swaying shuffle common to dancing here.

One or two of the people had come to show me sores, asking me to cure them. I doled out carbolised vaseline and similar remedies, with instructions, but probably they were taken internally.

At nightfall the negroes retired into the hut, and I could not accept Papa's offer to me of the hospitality of its overburdened stowage space. A mat and a waterproof blanket under the stars served me better. I rolled myself up, for the dew was heavy, but night brought no silence or cessation of speech. One or other of the crowd in the hut would waken at intervals; he at once waked someone else, and talked. All through the dark hours the chattering never ceased. Dawn was still sketched out in black and white when they arose and trooped out.

The old man at once sought his bench, and began his day-long vigil. A small, fat, black girl raked among the flaky ashes of the wood-fire, and soon collected a little heap of glowing red for the coffee. The gorilla boy brought me a cup of water for my ablutions, but I preferred the lake down in a valley about a quarter of a mile away. There you could bathe in shallow water, underneath which was a quicksand which took you to the knees.

By the time I returned, the day had grown into lemon colour, and a smell of burning coffee berries arose with the gouts of rich blue- black smoke from the fire. In the midst of the blossoming, fruitful land, this unsightly home was a fresh offence. About the huts small Haytians fronted the morning sun, naked and unashamed. The luxuries of life had no place here; necessity is the only queen in wild Hayti. Truly it may be said of man here that naked he comes into the world, and naked, using the term in its widest sense, he goes out of it again.

Of the peasant's attitude towards the stranger in the more remote districts, I have nothing to say but good. His virtue of hospitality is beautiful. His politeness is beyond reproach. He is Nature's gentleman in many ways, and though he is poor in worldly goods, he is rich in some of the higher qualities.

Riding through the rural districts you find it hard to obtain anything to eat, but easy enough to get a place in which to sleep. The people cannot give you what they have not, but they do give what they have, and that with both hands.

Even nearer to the towns I have known a peasant rise from his own bed, place sheets upon it, and lead his guest to it. If you offered him money-payment in the morning he refused it aggrieved, but a knife or some such trifle, presented as from one equal to another, was received with pleasure.

The average diet, if you except the fruits which grow of themselves, is limited to a little rice, sticky seed cakes with brown sugar, that make you sleep, and, if luck is good, sour bread. In mango season, they may say, as in Jamaica, "Turn up the pot;" while the fruit lasts there is no need for cooking.

Sometimes a pig is killed, one of the sharp-snouted, slabsided scavengers that are everywhere in evidence. A European digestion would infallibly fail before this special brand of pork, but the robuster negro appears to put it away without inconvenience.

Their relaxations are twain — dancing and cock-fighting. Their ideas of wealth take the form of the possession of these plumed warriors. But it is good to note that they have never heard of such barbarous things as steel spurs. The cocks are permitted to fight with such weapons as Nature has given them.

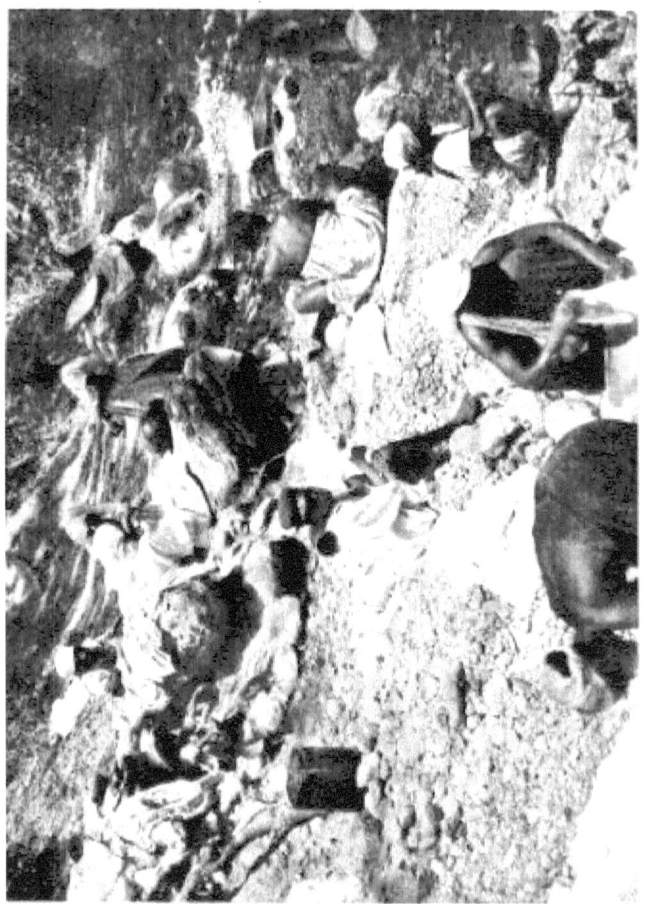

But the mountain people among whom Papa and his like reigned were not at all representative of the average native. They were a wilder race, with the shyness of the woods upon them, and what I have written above as to other districts must not be taken as applying to them. Here were no such civilised adjuncts as sheets ; life was raw, crude, rudimentary. Taken all in all, it was the sordid, purblind life of savages.

To-day in that lonely stockade was but a replica of yesterday, the one barren as the other. The old mumbling man sitting on the old bench, the large-headed, solemn child carrying him an ember for his pipe. Birth and death in scarcely-heeded sequence visited the hut, but the old man drowsed on. Fie reigned there amongst the dust, the sandflies, the hot wind, the parched tamarinds in the stale and rotting stockade, and his kingdom was only existence and the passage of hours. And there he will go on reigning until he goes out of a world that has already passed beyond him.

7

Into San Domingo

EVERY country has its own modes of travelling, more or less pleasant. In this tropical land you either ride through the heat of the day or you continue your journey far into the night, and if the night should happen to be starless your direction and your life are both at the mercy of your horse.

One night comes back to me above all others. I was in the far interior. The road ? There was no road. A track led round boulders, and branches hung low over it. You had to be careful of your eyes, for thorn bushes thrust out inch-long prongs to maul you. I was haunted by the fear of them. Think what blindness would be up there in those remote solitudes!

We were passing over the mountains beside Lake Assauei, and there was nothing to guide one through the forest, for in the sky was only the light of the evening star and a white moon in her first quarter. We had ridden many miles, and many more lay in front of us before any chance of rest or food. The so-called bottomless lake was on the left hand, the trail wound in and out about loafshaped hills crowded with forest and tangled with those inwoven creeping plants which one always associates with the idea of a South American jungle. The scent of the water was in the air. Stones shifting under the horse-hoofs supplied the dominant sound ; you heard them fall over the precipice, and long afterwards the echo of their plunge in the unseen lake came up feebly.

We were riding along a cliff, unable to see more than four yards ahead; my white horse was moving forward with a sort of irritable caution, feeling the trail. The guide, who had no taste for night-pioneering, followed on a shaggy mule.

Occasionally, by the light of your cigar, you could see a dark bush or a thick tree-limb close above your head. You dodged to evade it, and the thorns ripped away jagged strips of hat or coat. This sort of thing seemed to go on for hours. The forests, almost untraversed by man, certainly by white men, were silent save for the occasional movement of some bird, a wind in the leaves, or the pulsating fall of a stone as it struck the cliff-side on its long leap into the lake. You felt gigantically alone — in the heart of the Black Republic and the black night.

Presently it was certain we had lost our way; the forest raised up an impenetrable wall in front of us. We turned, and by the help of a series of lit matches tried to come upon the path again. This happened four times. Two hours later (by the watch — by one's feelings four at least) we began to descend towards the lake, where it was more likely we might come upon some stray hut. Our respective mounts leaped and scrambled and slid down tunnel-like declivities, over-arched with trees and paved by a water-cut lane, which lent itself to unexpected steep drops at frequent intervals. Riding of this sort would of course, be quite impossible in a country ranged over by big game, but here there is nothing more formidable to be met with than an escaped pig or a dog run wild. At length we came upon a solitary hut, where my guide managed to raise the materials for a torch.

And now it was that we reached the difficult part of the journey. The torch with its comet tail of sparks moved in the blackness like a red tracery on a ground of black velvet. The shadows made rushes at you as you swayed your light this way and that above your head. The horse kept his footing after the extraordinary manner of Haytian horses, despite the fact that the ground at his feet was a moving panorama of light and dark.

On, and on. and on, and the guide seems less hopeful than ever of the end of our ride. The truth is he has long ago lost himself. Finally, the torch burns itself out, and again we plod on at haphazard through a gully. The night grows in round us again. As we top the next incline a scream pierces upwards to us. We push on. Now you can hear the short, sullen bark of the Vaudoux drum, and, advancing from behind a curtain of black trees, in which are netted stars and fire-flies, we come in sight of a great red glow set in the heart of the forest.

A group of negroes are dancing round the fires; it is the wind-up of a three-days-long Vaudoux orgie. Two days ago a black goat was sacrificed to the sacred snake, and the frenzy of the worshippers is still unexhausted. There they are, screaming, writhing, and swaying, apparently blind to all outward things. You rein up your horse to watch. They take no heed of you, for they have no eyes in this remote and lonely spot save for their excesses. Here they are not afraid of interference: not that interference is to be expected anywhere in the island, but in these wild districts, cut off from civilisation and the towns by the slabby and unmanageable mud of the rainy season and by the pathless hills, they omit all precaution.

Easily you can pick out the Mamaloi. There she is in dirty white, bound round the waist with a red sash. Opposite to her dances a large, fierce-eyed, splay-footed negro. The fires, the posturing black forms, the uncouth howls — it is like a scene from Hell. You may be the bravest man in the world, but when you recollect that the probabilities are hugely in favour of these same people having sacrificed a child to their god at some date not too remote, your hand goes creeping to your revolver.

When you grow tired of watching, you turn and make a detour, skirting the far edge of the clearing, and, finding the track again, you pass through a deserted village, the inhabitants of which are all at the Vaudoux dance. The fires, which the negro always keeps alight, still shine, mere glow-worms on the bare brown earth.

While upon the subject of child-sacrifice, let me state that although there can be no doubt that at certain seasons of the year, and more particularly at Easter and Christmas, such sacrifices do most certainly take place, still, regardless of what has been written upon the subject, I strenuously believe that no European, with the single exception of one Catholic priest, has ever actually been present on an occasion of the kind. The dead child sacrificially dismembered has frequently been seen afterwards, but the actual ceremony excludes most rigorously all save the initiated.

The noise of the dance dies away behind. We are now in lower and marshier land. The young moon has set, the trees seem taller and tower up above us. Monkeys move restlessly in their branches, disturbed by our passing. The going on the mountains was bad, but this gorge is worse. The trees advance on you like a regiment in open order; you are swallowed up amongst them. A night's bivouac in the forest is all that we can look forward to. We are hopelessly lost and only day can deliver us. I mention this to the guide. He acquiesces. This is in fact the point towards which his diplomacy has all along been directed. Regardless of the chorus of frogs and the more than marshy ground, he proposes to bivouac on the spot, but the unhealthy chill speaks eloquently of malaria, and we move on.

NATIVE HUT ON THE WAY TO SAN DOMINGO.

A HAYTIAN HIGHWAY.

More quagmires, more boulders, more branch-dodging, more slipping of the tired beasts we ride. Will it never end ? At last we come to a possible halting-place, a deserted hut, with no walls, and a broken roof, its supporting posts scarred with flame. In the centre of the floor a heap of white and flaky ashes, the remains of a dead fire. You put your hand to it. A faint heat. Someone camped here last night. Probably a game-cock farmer from one of the Haytian villages, who was working his way eastwards to the good markets of San Domingo City or Barahona.

The guide rekindles the fire and fetches water from a stream, and you manufacture a meal of rice and soup in a tin mug. After that one pipe. Then you stretch your hammock between the joists of the open hut, and the next thing you know is that the light of dawn is filtering down into your eyes through the trees. You arise and take your bearings to find you have wandered four miles only out of your intended path.

Farther and farther we plunged into the doublings of the sierra, valleys closed up behind us, and hills folded in one upon another, and still we pushed on through the almost virginal forest. The trees above were dark against a sky where the morning stars shone together. Presently, as the woodland thinned away to more open country, a hot wind, bearing on it the exhalations of the marshes which fringe Lake Fundo, blew idly by.

Then all at once in the rising day you come in sight of the lake which is half in Haytian, half in Dominican territory. It is deep and still and blue, cradled in towering hills about which cling turquoise clouds, and the whole wide scene shines out upon you with a strange insistent beauty, the essential charm of which it is hard to analyse. A few plumes of soft grey smoke rise straight as palm stems from the other shore, and high up, lark-high in heaven, a breeze catches them and blows them abroad into great wisps and fronds that melt slowly out of sight.

Up on the mountain side the air is like champagne, cool and bracing. All around, from peaked summit to the water's edge, the forests spread in an unbroken sea of green — an uncalculated wealth of timber. A few trees are occasionally felled on the other side of the mountains, and in due time reach Port-au-Prince for export, but very little is done: absence of roads or of any means of communications dams up the riches of the country into the interior. The Consular Report for 1898 masses the export of mahogany with six other items under the remark: "Not of sufficient importance to be quoted!" Golden opportunities lie ripe to be plucked, but here is no hand to pluck them.

By the shore herons stalk through the shallows and show their awkward grey-blue bunch of body set between the angles of legs and beak. Alligators lie abask in the strong, sweet sunshine. The whole picture with its broad, vivid tones of blue and green is magnificently tropical and rich and high-coloured.

If the flag of any other country flew over the land, how long would this glorious lake and its fellow across the border retain their present opulent desolation? No boat pushes a venturesome forefoot through the brackish water —(for these lakes are salt, yet fed by fresh springs, so that here and there you can stand in salt water and drink fresh) -save one which American enterprise has brought with infinite trouble through the blocked-up land and set afloat on Fundo.

In the French times there were country houses here, but they lie in ruins, swarmed over by the ingrowing forest. I sought out the almost lost vestiges of a colonial estate. The fierce fingers of the tropic seasons had torn and twisted it into untimely decay; no doorways, no outline of living rooms, nothing but a heap of tumbled walls not as high as your knee, with lizards sleeping on the sun-warmed stones and forest vines tangled over their downfall.

It is the same all over Hayti wherever you go; all that savours of industry, energy, civilisation, in short, has been and is not. All that the white races left behind as milestones on the path leading up out of sheer savage waste and idleness is obliterated. As far as the interior is concerned, the situation in the present day is retrogression with regard to the human element, and retrocession to the forest-powers of once cultivated lands.

There you are among a people who prefer a thatched hut to a palace. The inhabitants scattered about that part of the country are few, but none of them have made their presence felt. A shanty of, so to speak, sticks and leaves buried in the trees is all you find. At the distance of fifty yards you are unaware of the presence. The land is empty but for a few birds and reptiles.

In the remoter places you may see a dog run wild, and breeding wild, slink with its litter from foliage to foliage ; or perhaps, when camping, a herd of pigs, also run wild and lacking the forked stick which is the domestic emblem, the sign of man's ownership, comes out upon you unaware and flies grunting to thicker cover. On Gonave Island wild pigs proper, descendants probably of those droves hunted by the buccaneers in bygone days, still haunt the recesses of the woods.

Late that night, as we came through a wilder defile than usual under the dark green forest shadows, a fire, small as a firefly, twinkled on a ledge above the track.

"Qui vive?"

A little ramshackle guardhouse, showing against a wall of trees, was perched on a clearing just big enough to hold it. It was of wood, rust-coloured and dreary-looking. Broken walls stood up awry from the floor of the forest, and on the narrow piazza in front two ragged soldiers, like a pair of vultures, craned over the road. They unslung their rope-suspended rifles and demanded passports. For this was the Frontier Guard of Hayti. They came down the slope of broken weedy ground until an arm stretched up from horseback could reach them, and examined the passports, and before they had recovered their places at the fireside and sunk back upon their haunches, we were over the border and in the Republic of San Domingo.

The Laguna de Fundo used to be entirely on Haytian territory, but now the Dominican landmark has moved slowly and ominously half-way up its blue waters. Even on the lake level the air was balmy, the temperature ranging from 90 degrees on the shore to anything you prefer on the rise of the mountain sides. Neither Cuba nor Jamaica can give you a climate so perfect as Hayti.

Evening came with a wind, and the lake was transformed. Seen from the lower ground it now appeared like a menacing eye, set beneath the rough and scowling brow of the mountain. No wonder legends have grown round about it.

The Laguna de Fundo and its companion, which its altogether within the limits of San Domingo, are both about 200 feet above the sea-level, and in times of heavy rains or floods are connected by water lying in the lowlands between. Lake Enquirillo, the larger lake, is supposed once to have been connected with the sea by a subterranean river ; the waters are salt, and it is said sharks and porpoises still exist in them; but to this last I cannot bear any personal testimony.

I remained in the Dominican State but a short time, and the little I saw of the people did not strike me too favourably. They are not nearly so likeable as the Haytian peasantry, and hospitality does not flourish in the same degree as on the western side of the border. On the other hand, the Government of San Domingo is lessjealous of foreign influence.

The Dominicans speak Spanish, and have preserved the purity of their language to a far greater degree than can be said of the Haytians, whose French has degenerated into a Creole patois so corrupt that it can with difficulty be understood by outsiders. A reason for this may be adduced from the fact that in San Domingo we find a coloured as opposed to an entirely black population.

NATIVES.

For San Domingo is the Mulatto Republic, and the mixture of races has probably done much towards keeping the general status of its people on a higher level; yet the lack of energy is very apparent there also. There is no doubt that both States contain a vast amount of mineral wealth, of wealth of all kinds, but the output is blockaded hopelessly by their respective Governments and the inertness of the people.

The trail into San Domingo is little travelled. A few natives work across to sell fighting-cocks, a few more have an interest in cutting wood beside the lakes, a few who have committed misdeeds break cover there for safety. For the rest there is no traffic ; it is left to the parrots that fly above and the wild pigs which range in the woods.

And this, you must understand, is the chief highway between Hayti and San Domingo.

In the time of the late Dominican President Hereaux, who was assassinated some months ago, there used to be a few soldiers posted on the frontier, but either Jimenez recalled them or they have recalled themselves. If a history of Hereaux comes to be written, I think the lie will be given to many superficial observers who have committed their ideas upon him and his methods of ruling to paper and added praise. It is hard to believe that certain of them had any personal knowledge of the man or of his country. Here was a ruler masterful certainly, but whose mastery was obtained by the foulest of means. He was a President of the Central American type, unscrupulous, pliable, fair-seeming, and immutably vengeful.

8

Haytian Police, Prisons, and Hospitals

HE was lightly attired in the remnants of a striped shirt, and what the passage of years had left of a pair of skyblue cotton trousers. On his head he carried a blue cap with a red band, and in his hand a dirty yellow club. He was a very black and lowering negro, with the invariable scanty imperial on his chin, which accentuated the resemblance that sprang at once into my mind — a humanised black goat.

I was told that he was a policeman of the Republic, and experience afterwards substantiated the fact that he was quite a fair sample of the force.

They are like no other police all the world over; they stand curiously alone in respect of many particulars. When on duty they loaf about the streets, and are very frequently fulfilling their duties in a manner that you are glad to

escape from witnessing. Elsewhere one seldom sees the colour of human blood ; in this island the chances are that you will see it flowing in broad daylight whenever the guardians of the peace think fit to make an arrest, for they are prone to use their coco-macaque clubs, and in the cases where the victim is not picked out at random as a medium whereby they may secure a meal, they are sure to be beating the wrong man.

The police are merely soldiers told off casually for the maintenance of the public safety. Their pay is ordinarily in arrears, and when remitted to someone in authority for distribution, reaches them in an attenuated form. In addition to this, they have to "keep themselves," but the administration has invented an ingenious method by which a truly zealous officer can manage to stave off" starvation very well indeed.

In some towns, at any rate, they receive a capitation fee of fifty centimes — a fluctuating sevenpence-halfpenny according to the exchange — for every man they arrest. Fortunately, living is cheap, so that when hunger bears too hardly upon them the remedy of a timely prisoner is easily come by. There need be no superfluous scruples, such as waiting until a man commits an offence against the law. Pick a quarrel with any stray passer-by or pounce down upon him unawares. There will be some howls and a patter of flying feet as the victim understands his ill-luck, and flies from it.

But the policeman is not to be so easily baulked; he bounds in pursuit. Perhaps the pursued doubles, and catches a thud on the shoulder from the cocomacaque club. With a cry, he rushes in to close with the policeman : in every arrest I witnessed the procedure was the same — the two struggled for possession of the club.

Not for long, however. A sleeping policeman reels into wakefulness up the hot street, and rushes out with flying coat-tails from the nearest arrondissement. " Tenez, tenez!" he shouts, as he makes to the aid of his companion, and smash goes his club on the head or face of the offender, who lets go his hold, and the first accuser takes the opportunity to indulge in a thorough-going revenge. The victim is taken away to the lock-up afterwards in a more or less unspeakable condition.

If he were a white, one would say, knowing where he is going to, that he must die of his injuries. As he is black, the chances are that after some days of pain he will recover from the beating. The back is suited to the burden, says the proverb; also in Hayti the thickness of the skull to the stick. The cocomacaque club is a cane jointed like a bamboo, but solid and unbreakable. It is heavy enough to fell an ox, and it is used indiscriminately over the heads and bodies of the prisoners. It is iron shod to add piquancy to the blows. Even the negro occasionally succumbs to its powers, and has been known to die by the roadside on his way to the jail.

The cocomacaque, like the policeman, is indigenous to the Black Republic.

I cannot take an example of this singular method of action from the contemporary newspapers of Hayti, as they rarely, if ever, print news of this sort, either because such occurrences are too common to call for comment, or they are too wise to mention what is in the nature of a grave scandal. But formerly, when a more independent paper existed, cases like the following were duly published. Sir Spencer St. John, British Minister in Hayti, quotes from "La Verite" of August 23rd, 1887: —

" A Death in Prison. — Our readers may remember that the individual who had tried to pillage the house of M. Marmont Flaubert had been wounded by the police : he was taken to prison in this state. His leg was horribly fractured. From want of attention mortification soon set in, and presently the existence of this unfortunate was in peril. A good woman, of whom a few are still found among us, overcoming her repugnance, wished to assist him in his last moments. She tended as well as she could the putrid limb, and talked of God to the dying wretch. He was touched, sent for a priest, and confessed with every sign of sincere repentance, received extreme unction, and died quietly shortly after imploring Divine mercy."

Another example : — "On Sunday, about eleven o'clock at night, two countrymen who were not sleepy were amusing themselves playing with dice or cards under the gallery of a house in Courbe-street. The patrol arrived. One of the young men bolted and gained the courtyard where he was accustomed to sleep. The other was not so prompt : he is caught: a blow from a cocomacaque stops him. Struck on the nape of the neck, he fell dead without uttering a cry. No means of passing this unfortunate off as a thief." -(July 1 6th, 1887.)

Other instances could be given, but these suffice to show the shameful licence permitted to the police in Hayti, and their wanton brutality. Such cases are sufficiently horrible, and I adduce them to show what another Englishman — one who was not only on the spot to judge for himself, but who also took the trouble to verify details, — has said upon the subject.

He bears ample witness to the state of affairs several years ago, and I can add on personal observation that they continue to be in precisely the same condition to-day. During my second walk through the streets of Port-au-Prince I came upon a Haytian scene of arrest. I need only say that the prisoner had been so cruelly battered that a gentleman passing offered the police a dollar to take the wretched man to gaol without further man-handling. For answer they attacked him again with their clubs. The man was a soldier who had omitted to turn up to drill because he was doing some work to earn a few centimes to buy food.

On another occasion I saw a captain of police called in by a negress who had attempted to steal from a store. The owner of the place, a Danish subject, naturally interfered to save his goods. The woman went out and returned in a few moments with the police officer, who threatened to shoot the Dane, and then stood by while the woman, under the protection of his revolver, wreaked her vengeance with a heavy stick. The upshot of this case, when brought into court, was a sentence of imprisonment on the Dane, with the option of a heavy fine.

At the time of arrest white men are mostly exempt from violence, although there have been several exceptions. But the negro, whether guilty or only under suspicion, or, as I have shown, really innocent of any offence against the law, is liable to murderous treatment both at the time of arrest and afterwards in the prison itself.

Moreover, the condition of the prisons all over the country is almost incredible when one considers that they exist in the midst of a community that calls itself civilised. I am well aware that the curse of the present police and prison systems is a source of shame and regret to every Haytian who has the good of his country at heart. Many have spoken of the matter to me, but the Government appear to be entirely indifferent.

A little brief authority is poison to a negro, whose inflated vanity is not tempered by education and whose intelligence seems too dwarfed to afford him any adequate idea of the pain he inflicts. One can only account for it on the supposition, which close acquaintance with the race certainly goes to support, that negroes have far duller nerves and are less susceptible to pain than Europeans. They recover from injuries that no white man could hope to survive, and that without tendance or medical aid of any kind.

The policeman still strides through the land in the name of Liberty, Equality, and Fraternity. Within the limits of his office he has absolute power, and this absolute power is placed in the hands of a man the mysterious workings of whose mind leads him occasionally to shoot his prisoner, not while resisting arrest, but afterwards for having resisted it! It is scarcely surprising that few negroes from other countries become naturalised Haytians.

Realism, as some understand the word, can be studied with effect in the prisons of the Black Republic.

To begin with, the prisoner, as has been said, usually enters jail suffering from maltreatment more or less severe at the hands of his captors. He is flung among his fellows into a narrow courtyard to live or die, as destiny and the strength of his constitution may decide. No tendance of any kind is given to him, whatever his condition, nor does the State provide him with any food. He begs from casual visitors, or his friends bring him provisions when they can from time to time.

The date of his trial in the courts is vague — persons are now in the jails whose very crimes are forgotten, but there they still remain — the police or soldiers in authority keep him in subjection according to rough-handed customs of their own. There is no power to which he can appeal, for no one has the slightest interest in his fate. Justice and mercy are alike denied to him — he is helpless.

So you will find men in the various prisons of the island herded together under conditions which would disgrace the worst cattle-boat that ever crossed the Atlantic. I have seen them myself in more than one jail starving, dirty, suffering, without the barest elements of sanitation in their surroundings.

The prison of Port-au-Prince is situated in the middle of the town. The high, pinkish walls are set on the top with broken glass. It is divided into courts, some containing political prisoners, others the common criminals. A narrow door, through which you are obliged to pass sideways, admits you.

When I entered, the General of the prison was sitting cleaning his nails. His noble name I did not gather, although I was duly introduced to him. He told me that I could not see the prison unless I had a pass from the Minister of the Interior. I had not a pass, and knew excellently well that I could not obtain one, for the Black Government, though they take no care to cure the sores of the body politic, are careful to cover them from the public gaze. And the prison of Port-au-Prince is a sore indeed.

I pressed my request, but it was explained to me that the law wisely forbade the visits of strangers, as they not infrequently brought messages for the political prisoners. Finally, I put forward a plea which procured me the permission I wanted.

Under the guidance of a soldier, I was led away to the left, where round a large enclosure prisoners live in sheds. This was the best part of the prison, as I soon found out. The men had little articles to sell. I asked my guide what crimes they were guilty of. All sorts of things — uttering false money, theft, and murder.

"Why are they here, while others are so much worse off?" I asked.

"They pay for it."

It was only by sheer perseverance that I at length looked in upon the quarters which the Government provides for the poorer sort of malefactor. It is difficult to choose words to describe this noisome place. Here men live like dogs, and on occasion die like dogs also. I believe they are carried away when they are dead, but that is the sole sanitary precaution taken.

Doorless cells were round the walls, with straw upon the earth as in cages for wild beasts. Some prisoners were practically naked; a few had converted worn-out jackets into loin-cloths; all were in the last stage of destitution. Men, in iron anklets with a short chain between, stood or squatted round. All shades of colour were there, from yellow ochre to coal black, and everyone looked half-starved. Not a few had gaping wounds, and others were wearily ill, their backs furred with sickness and neglect.

In the centre of the court there was a filthy pool, and pigs rooted about amongst the accumulations of all sorts which strewed the ground. Hercules cleaned the Augean stables; I scarcely know how he would have faced a task such as Hayti could offer him here.

In this part of the world they do not provide political prisoners with every luxury short of freedom. On the contrary, they are frequently chained to a bar in the clothes they stand up in, and it is not impossible to see a gentleman in a black frock-coat tethered by the legs.

Escape from the court where the rabble are confined seemed to be childishly easy, but the negro lacks enterprise. As in freedom, so in confinement, he takes the world as it comes. There are several hundreds in Port-au-Prince prison, and it is rightly regarded as a hotbed of disease.

Later on I visited another large gaol in the north at Cap Haytien. There also, as has been said before, the conscientious seeker after realism, upon whom perhaps the slum miseries of London have begun to pall, would find not only the hunger, the crowding, the disease, and the misery reproduced, but withal an indescribable residuum calculated to titillate the most jaded experience. All prisons in the Republic have the same essential features, and it is no more than a necessary precaution to take quinine before going on a tour of inspection.

In Cap Haytien as in Port-au-Prince the prison was divided into two chief sections, one for the civil and one for the criminal cases. There were 130 of the former and 280 of the latter, all dwelling in the stifling heat of two uncleansed, roofless yards. One man I spoke to had been awaiting trial for four months, another for three years.

It is hardly possible to imagine a white man imprisoned under such conditions of horror, yet, of course, it sometimes happens. For instance, if you have the misfortune to have your house burned down, there is a law in Hayti which regards it as a criminal offence.

A gentleman living in a certain town was consigned to the criminal side of the local gaol on this charge until investigation should be made. By making representations he had himself removed to the civil side, where, after a little time, he fell ill. The doctor supposed to be attached to the prison did not visit him. He became worse, and was at times delirious, but his request to be allowed to see his own doctor was steadily refused.

When the prison doctor did chance to come in, he saw that my friend was very likely to die, and knowing that this event might produce unpleasant complications — seeing that the prisoner was not a Haytian — he ordered him to be taken to the military hospital, which is little better than the gaol. At length, on payment of fifty dollars, he was allowed to be moved to the Hospice, where he was nursed back to life by the Soeurs de la Sagesse, a French sisterhood whose gentle care is the only tendance the sick can procure. Five hundred dollars in lawyers' fees was subsequently paid by the late prisoner. All this, in addition to the loss of his house and property, on account of an accident for which he was not in any way responsible !

In course of time, I visited the Military Hospital, a place chiefly distinguished by the absence of everything that goes to make a hospital — cleanliness, comfort, nurses. In the dreary shed which goes by that name patients and attendants were represented by a man lying on the earthen floor, suffering from a broken leg, and a negress smoking a pipe on an upturned tub by the doorway.

It seems impossible under black government for any undertaking or institution to be cared for, or kept up, or carried on. Some individual, in an ambitious moment, makes a start, but the beginning of any enterprise whatsoever is also the end ; no one bothers to go on with it.

The Hospice Justinien at Cap Haytien is, however, under French management, eight Filles de la Sagesse, who have

devoted their lives to the cause of Haytian humanity, taking charge of it. It stands on the edge of the Champ de Mars, fronting the blue, sun-scorched bay.

Crossing from the Military Hospital, I entered the Hospice, and was met by a nun, in a cool grey habit, her pale face almost as white as the starched wimple which framed it.

She led me up a flight of steps into a piazza, 70 or 80 yards long, grey-shuttered and shadowy, with whitewashed pillars and full of wandering winds. In the chapel some function was in progress, and the faint sound of chanting reached us. As I listened, heat, glare, dirt, and Hayti faded, and I was back: for a moment in another land.

Long rows of black bedsteads, furnished with sheets spotless as snow, lessened away into long perspective. Few of them were occupied, and by one or two sat doleful figures that to all appearance would occupy their places on earth but a few days longer.

"Oh, massa, I am very ill!" said one to me in English, and her face broke up. " And, oh, massa, I shall die here in the quiet "

She was a Jamaican negress.

Presently I was taken through a variety of rooms to the little chapel, where an old priest's fragile hands were raised from his black cassock towards the cool white roof.

Thence on through the men's ward, the women's ward, and out among the sick on the piazza.

"What is the matter with him."

The kindly-faced nun looked up at me and made a gesture with her hands.

"This, that, everything,'" she replied; "they have terrible diseases here in Hayti."

The man was sitting on a bed with a cloth over his head. He raised it as I spoke. He had no face, nothing save teeth and a few red strips of flesh.

"Poor creatures!" the nun said softly; "here, at the worst, they can die in peace. We help them to pass their last hours, if we cannot help them back to health."

The Haytian easily thinks himself sick, and takes his physic with the greatest appreciation. The more he swallows the greater his enjoyment. Here was one man who told me his head ached, and very black his face looked against the purity of his pillow. A fat little youngster was laughing and romping, riding a broom-stick up and down along the piazza.

After that I visited the well-ordered garden. Vegetables, fruit, and flowers of all climes — a place of green fragrances.

The Hospice is supported by private subscriptions, and deserves to be well maintained, for it is the only haven for the sick in a country where illness bespeaks little care for the sufferer.

I was told that rich patients were admitted, who could be at-tended by any doctor they chose ; for the poor the Hospice provided all medical treatment.

When at last I passed out from under the broad shadow of the front piazza under the palms, I went dreaming. The cool and the peace and the silence and the cleanliness and the purity, the echo of Latin song — it might have been another far-away home of nuns burled in green Breton woods.

All that I saw in the Hospice was so entirely the opposite of all that you find everywhere else in Hayti.

"Is monsieur pleased?" my guide asked me as I left.

I told her that it had been a rest even to see the place.

She bowed to me with a quaint courtesy, and so we parted.

The nominal religion of Hayti is Roman Catholic. It is the religion of the State, and an archbishop and four bishops are supposed to be paid by a grant from the Republican budget.

Up to 1860, when a concordat with Rome was signed, the condition of the Catholic clergy in the island was a source of scandal. So-called priests, whose "creed was need," set themselves up in the various parishes. But all that was altered forty years ago. Yet the process of evangelising the island goes on but slowly. Vaudoux has a strong hold upon the people. Its mummeries and horrors attract them, and a well-defined fear lies at the root of all.

The Catholic priests have a hard life of it, whether in the unhealthy suburbs of the towns or travelling through the mountains under a tropical sun, at one season choked with dust, at another drenched with torrential rains. These hardships, joined to the inadequate food which alone can be obtained in the country districts, brings down the average length of life to a deplorably low figure.

One of the numberless difficulties which lies in their way is the absorption of some points of their teaching into the mummery of fetishism. For instance, I have myself seen the sign of the Cross made on the forehead with the blood of a goat sacrificed to the snake-god. In the absence of the priest some of the chapels in which they are wont to celebrate mass have been used for the rites of snakeworship. The Papalois, the arch-priests of the cult, refer to the priests of Catholicism as brother ministers. Yet the Papalois are jealous of Catholic influence, and do all in their power to undermine it.

When you consider that no priestcraft has so strong a hold over a semi-savage people as that which can aid its votaries in the affairs of this present life, you will see why it is that snake-worship should be so serious a rival to Christianity. The Haytian naturally prefers a religion which not only permits but abets him in vengeance, which aids him to strike secretly at his enemy with poison. Here, indeed, the negro feels that reward is not shadowy, that he is getting his money's worth.

For these reasons Christianity labours under considerable disabilities in the Black Republic. Nevertheless, the Republic owes much to Christianity: all charity, all self-sacrifice, all care for the sick in Hayti spring from that source.

But since the Catholics do so much for Hayti, is it not inconsistent to fix the marriage-fees so high that the peasant cannot afford to marry? These fees amount to many dollars, as much perhaps as a peasant-farmer can make in the round of the year.

The natural result is that for every married couple there are 50 couples " places," as they call it. There is no need to say more on the subject. It speaks for itself.

Hayti boasts of its religious toleration, nor is it an empty boast. Many sects of Protestants not only exist, but are encouraged in their efforts to evangelise. One writer whose articles had something of a run in Hayti speaks of the Protestants as follows : " Let us try to Protestantise the country . . . the Protestant is economical, respects the law, loves reading, is a friend of peace, rich in gallant hope and perseverance . . . The nations that are dreamy, sleepy, imaginative, easily discouraged, depressed, are Catholic. . . . All who engage in commerce, agriculture, manufacture, progress, enrich themselves, prosper, are Protestants." Yet it cannot be said that Protestantism makes any way in Hayti.

I have referred in a former chapter to an instance, the only one, I believe, on record, when human sacrifice was actually beheld by a white man. The witness was a young French priest whom Sir Spenser St. John met at the palace of the Archbishop in Port-au-Prince.

This young cure had persuaded some of the people to take him to a Vaudoux service. They blackened his face and hands, and disguised him as a peasant. After a prelude of the usual frenzied dancing and whirling, a cock and a goat were sacrificed.

Later on, one of those present knelt and prayed the Mamaloi to complete the sacrifice by the offering of the "goat without horns." Upon this a child was disclosed, sitting with its feet bound. As the Papaloi approached the victim with the knife, the child screamed aloud, and the young priest rushed forward, shouting "Spare the child!" He was at once surrounded by his friends, who smuggled him away.

On his return to the town he tried to rouse the authorities, but they would do nothing until the morning, when on going to the spot they found the remains of the feast and the boiled skull of the child. No action was taken against the criminals, but the priest was deported under the excuse that it was dangerous for him to remain in the neighbourhood.

There are undoubted difficulties in the way of evangelising Hayti.

9

A Living City Within a Dead One

WHEN I reached Cap Haytien revolution was in the air.

The " Olinde Rodriguez" came to anchor, and I went ashore —
to be received as a conspirator.

I could not conceive the reason, but the fact remained that I,
the correspondent of the "Daily Express," landing in Cap Haytien,
produced all the effect of a stone falling into a pool of shrimps.

When I arrived they were expecting a Minister; the troops and
Generals, in about equal numbers, had turned out in full gorgeous-
ness to meet him. Drums were beating and flags were flying, but
when it became known that the expected grandee had not put in an
appearance the military and the twenty-seven mounted Generals
took themselves off.

As I had come from a port within the borders of the Republic I hardly expected any trouble with the Customs, but herein I
found myself mistaken. My light baggage was pounced upon by a
tall soldier, and, in spite of remonstrances and protestations, was

carried into the presence of a gold-laced General, who ordered me to open it.

I explained that coming from Port-au-Prince my effects were not liable to inspection.

"Have you letters?"

" Certainly."

"Give the letters to me."

The scene had shifted towards the door into the sunlight, and a crowd of guffawing negroes gathered to superintend the discomfiture of *le blanc*. An assistant of the General's rummaged through my belongings until he came upon the MSS. of these papers and a few private letters, which things were clearly suspicious and produced a profound sensation.

The General seized them. "What has *le blanc* got here?"

I explained that I was in the habit of keeping a diary of my daily doings. My private letters were impounded on the spot. Searching questions were then put to me concerning my name, my destination, and my business in the Republic. Soon an official informed me that I was at liberty to go away. This was not to be thought of, as I knew in my heart that, with my manuscript, I was leaving my liberty and, possibly, my life behind me; for Hayti is a country in which it is by no means healthy to write down exactly what the traveller may see. You must not under any circumstances express a political sentiment, least of all, ye gods, on paper! Why, only the other day a gentleman of sporting tendencies shouted " A bas President Sam" in the street at Port-au-Prince. A negro guard leaped out of the shadows and shot him dead. I remembered this also, that no English Consul existed within two hundred miles of me.

There was nothing for it but to produce my Foreign Office passport and to speak vaguely of my position as a British subject and the long arm of the British navy. I talked of the "Powerful" and the "Terrible." They whispered together, and, after a considerable interval, returned my notes. May the shadow of the British Empire never grow less!

The official activity was afterwards made clear to me. An ague-fit of revolutionary hankerings had swept across Northern Hayti, and at the time I chanced to arrive the Government were still keeping a wide-open eye on all correspondence. With my MSS. in my kit I lived on without having attained to either the picturesqueness or the inconvenience which inevitably attach to a political schemer. But let us explore Cap Haytien.

They say that your outlook, or perhaps I should say your inlook, upon a country is largely influenced by the door through which you happen to enter it.

Hayti is no exception to the rule. Her three gates of ingress present each of them a definite and characteristic feature.

That of Port-au-Prince is dirt. That of Jacmel is fire-scorched and gutted black interiors. But Cap Haytien is a mushroom town of wood, built among imposing stone ruins.

Go in whatever direction you like the sights that meet you are the same. Ruined houses, ruined aqueducts, ruined fountains of stone, ruined walls, ruined forts. She bears upon her the indelible impress of the tremendous earthquake of 1842. From the sea the town is but a little cluster of dwellings heaped together beneath the wooded mountains in the corner of a big purple plain. Her jetties are broken, black, and old ; the usual wreck lies ashore in her harbour — there is one in the harbour of every important port in the Repubhc — but once ashore you are in the cleanest and the best kept town in all Hayti. The principal street fronts down almost directly on the harbour; it is wide and perhaps two miles long. Once in the old French days the town was the centre of luxury and fashion. It was called the "little Paris" of the West. Since then ruin and devastation have swept over it.

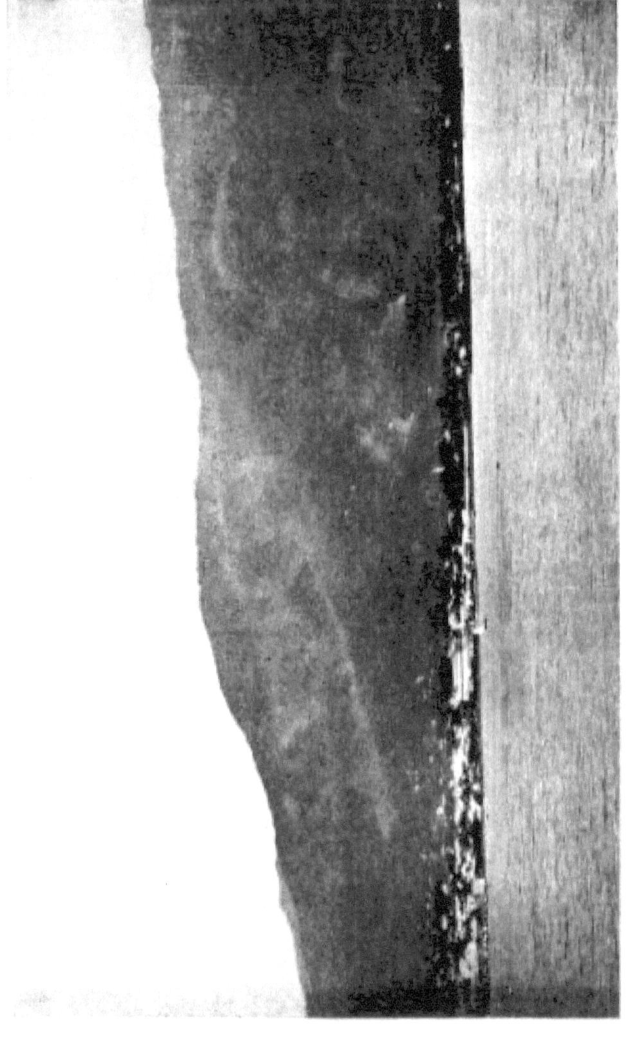

Half the hillside was torn away by the shock which annihilated the city. The dread earthquake shook down or seriously injured almost every house, two-thirds of the inhabitants were buried beneath the fallen masonry; bands of blacks rushed in from mountain and plain, not to aid in saving their wretched countrymen, whose cries and groans could be heard for two or three days, but to rob the stores and houses, while the officers and men of the garrison, instead of attempting to keep order, joined in plundering the small remnants of what the surviving inhabitants could save from the tottering ruins. What a people!

An American journaHst is said to have heard the above story of the earthquake and the looting of the town. His comment was: "My aunt I What copy for any duck who happened to be browsing around!"

To-day Cap Haytien is like a sparrow's egg laid in the deserted nest of an eagle. Wherever you walk you are among old ruins, knee high and over-grown. Among them have cropped up the wooden dwellings of the present masters of the land. The hills which back the town are guiltless of human habitation. Away to the north, guarding the harbour mouth, is Fort Picolet, garrisoned by two soldiers. It contains a few old cannon, which lean their black nozzles over the ruined parapets like a colony of basking seals.

It is a common saying in the Republic that no revolution can be successful unless it emanates at the Cape. It was the seat of Government under the Emperor Christophe, that terrible and masterful figure, to the days of whose iron rule the greater virility, energy, and enterprise of the population of the north are often attributed.

The town itself is well laid out, its cobbled streets are the cleanest I have seen in Hayti;— not too clean, you understand, but still far in advance of those of the capital or pestiferous Jacmel. And the people are superior also. They work harder, the soldiers have straighter backs and less ragged uniforms. These things are in some measure due to General Nord Alexis, the head of the department. He is an old man now, but if all the officials of the Republic did her as good service as this high-handed old General the country would be a wholesomer and a happier land.

Spread in all the main streets are sail-cloths covered with coffee berries, whose shining green bears witness to their high quality. Wild-eyed men, with naked torsos, toil shouting under sacks of it; bearded natives (whose extraordinary likeness to the Riffs of North Africa forces itself upon you), driving carts drawn by four, mules, take it with an accompaniment of indescribable din to the wharf, and there another horde screams for possession of it. In the South you do not see men working like that.

And all this riotous life boils and struggles in the midst of the old dead city, within the broken shell of its fallen palaces and aqueducts and baths, whose walls have mostly sunk to the ebb-tide level of destruction, and are hardly more than ridges above the ground. Time and weather and the strong soft fingers of tropical vegetation are slowly wiping out the remembrance of them from the face of the earth. To-day an occasional Haytian will point out with pride the tin erection of the new custom-house, proudly marked with the name of the reigning President. The white man built a hundred years ago, the black builds now.

Apropos of the threatened revolution I have alluded to, an extremely frightened gentleman once presented himself at the British Consulate, and begged the Consul to advise him what course he had better pursue if there should happen to be — as was then most likely— and shooting in the streets. The Consul, who was used to Hayti, slowly stroked his beard.

"What should you do?" he said slowly. "If I were you, Mr. Blank, I should at once get out of the — ah — line of fiah"

Hayti is a chameleon. She has been a Republic, an Empire, then once more Republic, again an Empire, and now a Republic over again.

Her history is one gigantic patchwork of revolutions. Whatever she may be like when her political temperature is normal, she changes completely when it goes up a degree or two. With her rulers a few suspicions are enough to be magnified into an attempted revolution, and, when once her temperature reaches this fever point, strange things of many kinds occur. Having been a suspected conspirator myself, do I not write with the diploma of experience?

Everyone is interested in revolution tales. Here are some true ones from the best forcing-bed in the world for such productions. They are dramatic tales fitting this land of tropical skies, and pronunciamentos, and vengeful Presidents. But these stories are something more than true and dramatic ; they were once everyday occurrences. The following are selected at hap-hazard from a thousand such, and they all happened during the last two revolutions. The point to bear in mind is that they are pretty sure to happen again during the next; for once the delirium of political excitement and strife begins to take hold upon the people they break away from the leash of civilisation.

Upon the death of President Salomon the usual sanguinary struggle took place for the possession of power, and it was in the course of this struggle that the ominous and daring personality of General Dardignac forged to the front. He was an adherent of Legitime, who eventually seized the Presidential chair. Dardignac was a mulatto with an iron-grey moustache and determined eyes, bloodshot with staring through dust and sun.

Now Dardignac was one of those strong men who make more enemies than friends. On one occasion he was going north with troops on a Riviere steamer (she trades between the Haytian ports to this day). About dawn they put in for supplies at a little seaside town, and some fresh passengers came aboard. While breakfasting Dardignac heard on the deck above him two voices, one of which he had reason to know too well. It was that of a prominent personage nicknamed Rude Raide, who for public or personal reasons had crossed the designs of Dardignac in past days. The General went on deck.

"My friend," he said, "I have been looking forward to a meeting such as this for years."

Rude Raide turned green and made a feeble attempt to offer conventional greetings. Dardignac called his men.

"Tie him up!" said he, and went below to finish his meal.

When he returned the affair developed. He ordered the steamer to be stopped. Fire-bars were tied to Rude Raide's ankles, and with his own hand Dardignac shoved him overboard. Those who saw it say that Rude Raide wriggled down upright into the depths of the sea. Then Dardignac laughed aloud; it was his form of humour.

During the same revolution he fought a battle near Grand Saline; the casualties mounted up to heavy numbers on each side, which is not a very common characteristic of this internecine warfare. Seven prisoners were taken. Dardignac, seated in an arm-chair, ordered them to be brought before him. By his directions they were placed in a semicircle, and with a small Winchester he shot them one after the other from his chair with his own hand.

Very brutal, of course ; but there was another and a no less definite side to the General's character. He was a man of fantastic bravery. He is known to have captured one of the enemy's ramparts unaided, riding at it armed only with a cocomacaque club. He sat in full view upon the ramparts, being shot at (and wounded), until the last man of his following was in.

At another engagement he was wounded in the groin. To show his contempt of pain, he was in the habit of giving audiences while the doctor probed his wound, and more than once the last footfall of his retiring officers had hardly died away before he fainted.

The end of his career was tragic. He was shot by his own soldiers.

As for the lower class of Haytian, he fights in a revolution, and knows not why he fights. The leader has his stake in the contest, the soldier has none ; he merely runs the chance of losing all he ever possessed — his life. Be the President who he may, the private remains the same ragged, unfed private still.

From this standpoint a revolution is pathetic. Here are these ignorant soldiers fighting, reinforced by a rabble of wild peasants and vociferous wharf-side negroes, helping to turn things upside down, and to make that peculiar concoction— Haytian history — and getting no good out of it for themselves. So it goes on: always a few military operations, a good deal of promiscuous shooting in the street and round corners, with a great deal of talk ; and as an aftermath pronunciamentos, imprisonments, and a heavy bill of mortality within prison gates or against the arsenal wall.

The revolutionist, it is true, wears no gloves of mercy, but the negro is hard to kill. Somewhere about 1888 a bold vanguard, numbering some five men, marched into a village upon the banks of the Artibonite. The villagers, believing the main body to be close behind, fled. The famous five seized food and ate, maltreated women and children, and otherwise enjoyed themselves each after his kind. The village people, who were hiding in the woods, presently found out that the five men were unsupported, so they flocked back to vengeance. Two of the five they killed, two escaped, and the fifth unfortunate was taken prisoner. They cropped his ears as they cut a pig's, they cut the tip off his nose, they slit his mouth to his neck. To crown all they broke both his legs with musket balls, and threw what half an hour before had been a man into a cactus bush.

Meantime the two fugitives had returned to the camp, and on their representations a force was at once sent out to immolate that gentle village. When the butchery was over, groans were heard to issue from the cactus bush. They pulled out the wreck of a man. He recovered. It is hard to believe this story, but there is the scarred man walking about Port-au-Prince to-day.

I do not know whether anyone, allured by my description of the country, feels moved to emigrate to Hayti, there to carve out a career for himself. To such I make a free present of the following revolutionary prescription. In a revolution the theory for the individual is — go for your worst enemy, and go quickly, or you will find him coming for you. When you have killed him, send in the bill to whatever Government has come into power, and demand a reward for patriotism. It is by working on this simple principle that many big local reputations have been made in Hayti.

When first I arrived in the island the country was drifting pretty surely towards revolution. The people were starving and discontented. Exchange stood at 190, and all because the price of coffee had fallen. Then came the news that an outbreak of the plague in Brazil had scotched the export of coffee from that quarter, exchange leaped back to 120 and 110 in four days, and the Government was saved. Even the bubonic plague has its uses.

10

The Citadel of the Black Napoleon

I LINGERED on at Cap Haytien.

For days I had waited.

For days it had become my habit to gaze across at the citadel, which I had travelled the length of Hayti to visit. There it was, seeming small as a crow's nest upon its mountain peak far away across the plains.

For days word was brought to me that the journey was hopeless — it could not be attempted.

Why? The roads were impassable.

First, because the rain had increased the fords and flooded the lower-lying parts of the intervening plain.

Second, because the sun had dried the mud to the consistency of glue, and no horse could do otherwise than stick helplessly in it.

Lastly, because there had been more rain.

Then I saw my opportunity.

With Haytian volubility I was implored to wait a week, a month, a fortnight, until, at the least, the ground was passable.

Through the kindness of a gentleman to whom I am most deeply indebted, I secured a guide and set out.

That road! How shall I bring it before you? Take a farmyard, a thunderstorm, a horse-pond, a fat ploughedfield, mix them thoroughly, spread over with unwholesome green scum, and you have it. Here and there you came upon a pool of the consistency of porridge. A negro fell into one just outside a village ; it rose shoulder high upon him. You tacked along like a boat in a shifting wind. To my middle I was sopped in mud. Never before did I realise the beauty of the profession followed by those gentlemen who drive water-tight carts round London, gathering up fluid street-slime. And the mud smelt, hot, thick, marshy. Up to the waist I was a mudlark, above that I was spotted in black on my yellow khaki like an Ethiopian leopard.

The vagaries of the road irritated one. Across the level plain it took you meandering half a mile out of your way for every three-quarters you went forward. My first objective was Millot, where I was to pass the night. It was a pleasant prospect, that of sleeping wet to the skin, yet I knew it to be unavoidable, for my small change of clothes had sunk long since into a sticky and revolting mass.

My guide, Petit Col by name, on hearing that I was an Englishman, christened me John. "This way, John," he would say. And "John" followed meekly for a time, until he discovered that Petit Col was as innocent as himself of the geography of the quagmires. Then "John" led, encouraged by the shouts of his retainer. Through morasses, into sloughs, wading rivers of mud, you entered into the spirit of it after a time. " The muddier the merrier." As long as I did not fall bodily into a hole I ceased to care what happened. Yet the first splash which painted me black from ear to mouth had produced unseemly language. The sky above was cloudless blue, and the sunlight, scalding yellow on the road, made the black surface of the slime dance and steam.

Much in the same manner we were still toiling on when sunset found us. At last we came in sight of Millot, the halfway house to the citadel of La Ferriere, which was built at infinite cost of human life some eighty years ago by the black Emperor of Hayti, Christophe, or, as he loved to call himself, Henry the First.

Millot itself is but a collection of a few hundred huts regular as the ranks of a regiment. Armed with letters and permits I rode into the village at the rising of the moon. In the shifting lights the place reminded me of Broadway in the Cotswolds of happy memory. Over the huts a blue haze hung low under the china-blue reflections of the moon. This haze was made by the smoke of many fires, that winked and burned small in the distance as fireflies. Riding nearer, one saw black forms crouching on their haunches, and other black figures dancing in the glow. In some hut at the back they were beating a drum with the rolling booming finger-motion which has come from Africa. And through this blue fog it was necessary for the traveller to seek out the General de la Place, that local potentate who is about as absolute a monarch as the Czars of Russia used to be, but are no more.

The General was not at his house, a straw-thatched building, consisting of three rooms and a narrow brick-paved verandah. Nor was he at the little guard-house in the central street. So we must seek him away up the hill through the puffy blue haze.

"*Qui vive?*"" The challenge was slung at us, as it seemed, from nowhere.

"*Anglais.*" We moved forward to find a dozen soldiers seated by a fire in the gloom of a wall-less shed very like an English cart-house. They caught up their rifles and proceeded to ask our business with one voice. I mentioned that I wished to see the Général de la Place, for whom I had letters. ' As usual, they attempted to confiscate them, but upon one of their number spelling out the addresses they became polite. Endless chattering followed.

At last, weary of waiting, wet from the rigours of the road, I handed over my letters, and begged the officer of the post to inform the General that I should do myself the honour of calling upon him to pay my respects in the morning. Then I followed Petit Col down the hill to find some place wherein to sleep.

The morning came with a grateful smell of strong sweet coffee. Then it was on-saddle again after a tin-full of that same excellent coffee, and away, guided by a large-headed, thin-legged four-year-old, to pay my promised visit to the Général de la Place.

Now, the Général de la Place holds an authority from which there is no sort of appeal. This time I found him at home. I rode into his yard and dismounted, not without some qualms as to the possible failure of my expedition. The Government are very much opposed to permitting foreigners to inspect the fortress of La Ferriere, but they are diplomatic in their refusals. The General at Cap Haytien will graciously give you a pass, which the General at Millot invariably cancels. As all this had been explained to me before starting I was, naturally, apprehensive. For a long time no one had been allowed to see La Ferriére — was I going to be more fortunate?

The General was a large coal-black man, in a frock-coat of shepherd's plaid check and a cream-coloured military cap. He was most affable. The usual compliments and some polite remarks passed between us. He was, he told me, thirty-five years old, and I? I trusted him with the secret of my age, and we found ourselves at once on an excellent footing. In his remarks about the citadel he was vague. Afterwards I discovered the reason of the prohibition to visit it.

The Emperor Christophe is said to have died worth fifteen millions, and this hoard of treasure no one has yet discovered. But some time ago a man — his name is of no import — appeared at a

Cap Haytien gaming-table, and tempted luck with what ? Spanish doubloons 1 No less than that most romantic and piratical coin? He did not deny having discovered the treasure of Christophe. The Government heard of it. Hippolyte was President at the time, and Hippolyte sent for him.

"Confide in me," said Hippolyte, " and become a General!"

Lured by this tempting bait, the discoverer came perilously near to giving up his secret, but not quite. He was then sent back to the north to Cap Haytien, where the General made the mistake of threatening him. The limpet might have yielded to caresses, but the finger of force closed his mouth. He was put into prison, and there by every barbarous means they strove to wrench his secret from him. Yet ever he bore his tortures, and closed his mouth the tighter.

At length they set him free, and had his movements carefully shadowed, but with no result. Finally hundreds of soldiers were sent to excavate. These again failed to find a trace of gold, and there the matter rests unto this day. The discoverer is still at large with fifteen millions locked up in his inviolable silence. Strange, blood-stained, old-world money like to Kidd's treasures, which are said to be buried near by in the Haytian Island of Tortuga.

But to return to the Général de la Place. We exchanged cards, and from his I learned that he was "Général Anahim Amazan, Général de Division aux Armées de la République, Aide-de-camp honoraire de son Excellence le Président d'Haiti, Commandant de la Place et de la Commune de Millot." In poor exchange he read mine, which held nothing but my name. I shall always look back upon General Amazan with gratitude. Nowhere could you meet with more courtesy than he showed to the bedraggled wanderer who presented himself before him.

The Town of Millot.

THE PALACE OF SANS-SOUCI AT MILLOT.

The creator of La Ferriére has been called the Black Napoleon.
Black as the purest African blood could make him, and born a
slave, he yet showed himself, in the afterdays of his power, to be

possessed of a right royal taste for splendid architecture of the most enduring type.

The mountain upon whose crest the fortress of La Ferriére is built takes two hours of hard climbing to surmount. But you have evidences of Christophe's ambitions long before you arrive at it. He loved broad and spacious roads and noble vistas, and these he forced his people to hew out for him from rock and plain and forest. But they are gone now, wiped out of sight by those two remorseless dissolvents of the results of human labour, neglect and nature.

Riding out of Millot I saw what is left of the black ruler's chief Palace of Pleasure, Sans-Souci. He had many other handsome dwellings, country-seats scattered about the rich plain of the Artibonite, bearing names which smack rather of the East than of the West — "Queen's Delight," "The Glory," "The King's Beautiful View," and so forth. Sans-Souci is built on a rising ground at the apex of a narrow and lovely ravine, set between steep green hills. It stands a grey ruin of lost effort, among the waste of its fallen gardens. The solid line of stone steps leading up to it still remains, though green things are pushing between the slabs.

You look up into the face of the main building above. It is a pale and shattered face, and from some of its blank windows trees are growing outwards. But there is not a memory connected with it that could raise a regret or make you wish to perpetuate one single association. For the history of the Emperor Christophe's fourteen years of power is one unbroken record of self-seeking, corruption, and cruelty.

Yet the man must have had great qualities besides those which enabled him to make himself autocrat and tyrant over his fellows. He was curiously different from the mass of his race, who love idleness, who do not seem to heed squalor, and whose liking for gaudy personal adornment is grotesquely devoid of all sense of congruity ; whereas Christophe's representative in England told, not only of extensive public works, ravines filled up, mountains levelled, and public roads laid out, but also of the inlaid work and rare tapestry with which the Emperor's apartments were embellished.

Leaving Sans-Souci we began the climb upwards. I was accompanied, not only by my own guide. Petit Col, but by the military escort provided for me through the agency of the General. This escort consisted of one small soldier armed with a club.

Outside the village we met a murderer being taken to prison by one of the country police, who was, of course, also a soldier. The prisoner was pinioned by a rope tied tightly round his upper-arms, and his captor drove him along with vigour. The poor wretch was nearly naked, and miserably thin. He had been wounded in the face, and a few broken teeth showed under his swollen lips. I gave cigars to each of the men, but I have no doubt that the soldier who was armed with a rusty modern revolver with a handle of mother-of-pearl, smoked both.

After a long rough climb through the ever-thickening forest, we reached the region of the clouds. A hail rang down upon us from the thicket of trees overhead, and a six-foot negro, armed with a machette, dropped down from the heights above the track. His clothing was not in keeping with the bitter cold. It consisted of the remains of a pair of trousers, of which the thorns had had their will, hanging in tatters about his thighs, while a piece of blue shirting, adjusted for wear by holes for head and arms, completed his costume. This was the chief warder of the Black Napoleon's great citadel.

He and a companion, similarly armed and yet more sparsely clad, now led the way. All trace of a path was gone, and to reach the Citadel, which full in view, towered starkly up above us, grim and ruinous and red-stained with lichen and overgrowth — it was necessary to cut out a track through the close mesh of underbush and creepers.

Yet, if report speaks truly, Christophe was wont in his own day to drive up to his fortress in the mountains. The warder guided us by devious turns and with many delays, while he cleared away the encroaching vanguards of the forest, until at length at the outer bastions of the fort the trees stopped short. From under their shelter we plunged out into a blinding, hurtling cloud of rain, and waited, chilled to the bone, until the sense of sight should be vouchsafed to us again.

The guards of the Citadel, inadequately provided in every way as they are, would have a poor time of it were it not for the fact that the Government, jealous of the discovery of buried treasure, changes the men every month.

After a time the rain thinned, I urged my horse to frantic effort, and shortly we gained the comparative shelter of the guard-house. A log to sit upon, a mass of fluffy, flaky wood-ash, eloquent of a dead fire, and a broken tin roof, supported on posts, but wall-less as usual, which merely served to increase the chill of wind and cloud that shot and drove under it as through a funnel, made up the sum of barrack accommodation furnished by the Republican Government for its servants.

Personally I found that khaki, though all very well down below in the ports and on the plains, was not the ideal material for facing this fierce weather. While we waited on the pleasure of the storm, the wild warder had plucked an orange from a tree hard by, and was peeling it with his machette. I remember I could hardly see what it was when first he cut into it, and yet, before the coil of peel fell to the ground, the overhanging cloud had flicked away its tail and the mountain summit was bathed in yellow, opulent sunshine.

And then came repayment to the fullest.

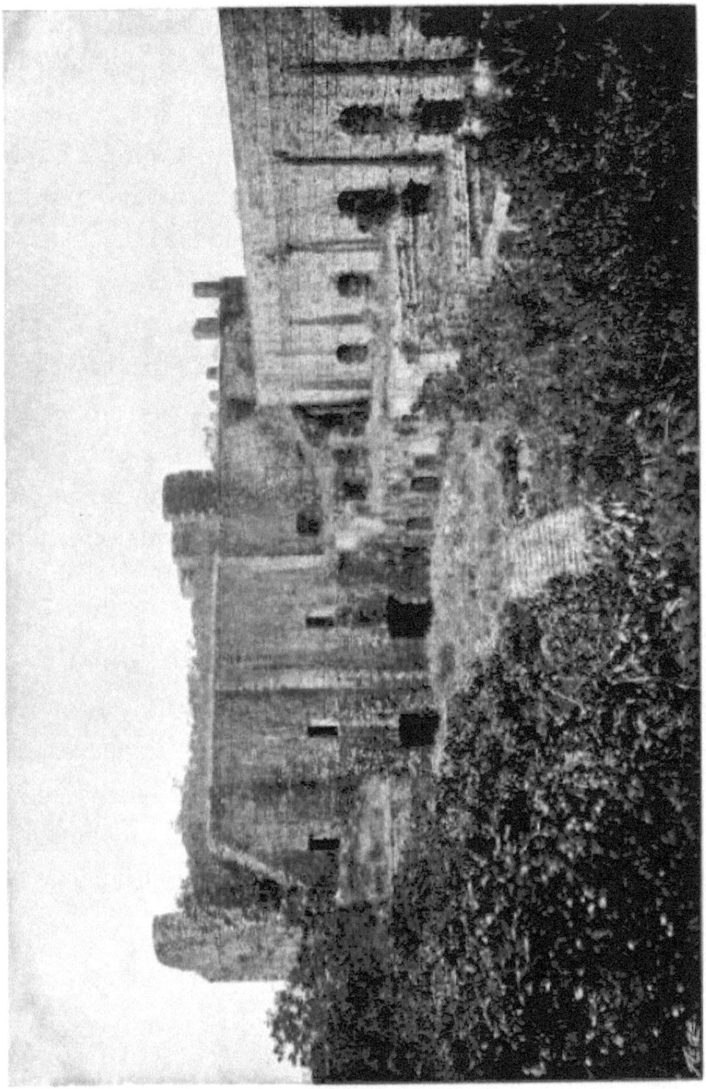

Interior of the Castle of La Ferrière.

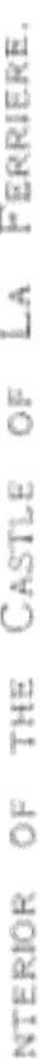

The whole green place laughed with a thousand dew-lit mouths. The trees dripped moisture and exquisite shades of colour from their low-hanging branches. Nature breathed warm in your face. You seemed to see her, savage and beautiful, flinging her unchecked arms about the great fortress as if to drag it down from its place of pride. Involuntarily I glanced up at the grim, walls, draped in their torn garment of orange-red mosses. Signs of decay and time show clearly enough upon them, yet they stand erect against the pale blue sky-line in impressive bulk. And then came that other contrast between the wild figures of the two warders and their great empty ward of solid stone and brick and masonry. They choose to live in their sordid dwelling-place, puny and tumble-down as it is, by force of race preferring it to the enormous ruin. Of that they were — afraid!

So it was; they were terribly afraid. Gingerly they opened the huge, nail-rusted, iron-bound door, pausing hang-footed on the vast threshold. For here ghosts move, they say, with shrill pipe through the blackness.

I gave the order to move forward.

But they held back. Something seemed to trouble them.

The four negroes gathered themselves into a little knot and gabbled together. Then one advanced and pushed back the creaking door. Old smells came out to meet us, and noises like giants laughing. It was only a landslip far away in the bowels of the mountain.

Well, we entered. I took three steps forward and a hand plucked me back.

I struck a match. A mouth of blackness gaped at my feet.

"Deep, deep I You dead if you walk there!"

After which I moved hang-footed too.

The great door of the ruin closed between us and the sunlight, and we were in the dark interior of the huge old citadel on Mont La Ferriére. Long deserted by man, and left to natural decay, its mighty structure shaken to dangerpoint by the violent earthquake of 1842, the Citadel is precisely the place where one prefers to walk by sight.

We groped our way up a flight of steps, and presently reached daylight again. We found ourselves in a long gallery, lit by narrow embrasures, each guarded by an ancient black-snouted cannon. There were nineteen of them, nineteen out of an aggregate of three hundred in the whole fort. Behind the cannon and all about the gallery were rolled and piled the rusty balls they were never destined to send forth. The flooring, as you moved over it, quivered like the bed of a snipe-marsh, and the place reeked of old wet smells.

Outside you could see the world alive and hot with glowing sunshine; here nothing stirred save the lizard startled from its bask. Of the long row of cannon some were of brass, and marked " Georgius IV. Rex," and some were strangely bearded with shining stalactites of pallid white, grown from the endless drippings of the roof. A little further on the floor did not look like bearing a heavy weight, so the lighter negroes went on alone like prying children, until ten yards ahead the rotten wood creaked and gave ominously, and they came scuttling back.

From the gallery we passed out into an open courtyard and the welcome warmth of the sun. Here, about the tomb of dead Christophe, the jungle, fought back and checked by the outer walls, has undermined them and broken out into fresh riot. Between the stems of the young tamarinds and through Guinea-grass head-high and higher, we pushed our way until we reached the resting-place, pink and age-stained, of the most dominant black in history, the negro who reproached Napoleon for surviving defeat, and who, true to his convictions, in the supreme moment chose death. In front of the tomb, under the covering slab, a hole had been broken through the masonry; inside it looked like a rabbit-earth where dogs had been scratching. Close over it from an orange tree hung fruit in ripe golden clusters.

Petit Col, the guide, stooped down and burrowed in the opening, and drew forth something yellowed, curved, and furred, — a human rib.

"Take it — Christophe," he said briefly, and diving again, plucked out what seemed to be a finger-bone. I declined the souvenir. It was a little too grisly. But the tall warder had no such scruples. He wrapped it in what served him for a shirt, for it was saleable. In the loneliness of the stark interior he would, I think, have shrunk from the act, but here he had company and the sunlight to stiffen his courage.

We plunged again into the jungle of Guinea-grass, and the men cut a path to some broken steps ; then, after passing through one more dark passage, we emerged upon the battlements. They are flat and wide enough for a carriage to drive along. From them one gains some notion of the vast thickness of the walls, fifteen to twenty feet of solid stone-work. Below, the whole plain spread out in gigantic bars of colour. The foreground of deep potato-green, dotted with huts small and black, like ranked dominoes, the distances fading into smoky grey, and far to the left the sea in a band of gleaming blue underscored the horizon.

It is not until you look suddenly straight downwards that you realise you are two thousand feet sheer above the plain. Two thousand feet — it does not seem very much in print, but when the eye follows the clean drop of grey wall and cliff to dim depths below, you become aware that the words have a pregnant meaning. A red moss creeps like old blood-stains about the stones. Here a few inches under the edge each minute feather is distinctly visible, a little further down you have a wide-spread blur, lower, lower, and lower, till the distance grows brown and your head reels, for at last the field of view comes up to you with a wavering sea-floor glimmer through the fathoms of air.

Old blood-stained walls in fact, are these of Christophe's Citadel. From the battlements men have leaped into space at his order, or been flung screaming out into the shuddering emptiness. The stories of his cruelty are endless. You wonder why the people submitted to tyranny they could have shaken oft", until you recollect that the will of a strong man usually holds the key to any situation.

A stone dislodged under the hand tumbled over the edge, and we hung breathless to hear it strike bottom. After we had ceased to listen an echo rose faintly upwards and surprised the ear. In due time we went back to the massive chill and silence of the ruin. Through the King's chamber, the Queen's chamber, and the dining-hall, a lofty, round, be-windowed place. While we loitered there, the sun went out as before. Billowing, smoky cloudwreaths came vomiting in through the blank windows, and threw us into a sudden twilight. It occurred to the wild warder to choose this juncture as a fitting moment to tell me something of the habits of the local ghosts.

"A ghost, if he can hurt you, looks at you and you die," he muttered; "the first time he comes he looks only at his feet, and the second time he is looking down, down at his feet; the third time he looks at you" — he flung up his two large-jointed hands with a gesture that depicted sudden death, and left very little to the imagination.

When, after some minutes, the cloud rolled off. Petit Col looked up. "There is nothing more to see," he said.

But I explained that the Emperor Christophe was not the man to leave out those old-time necessities, dungeons; and those all-time necessities, wells, from any building with which he had to do.

I was not disappointed in finding the Citadel dungeons quite up to the quality of their best European prototypes. The bottle-necked variety appears to have appealed especially to Christophe's practical mind. He had constructed four of them in a row ; each one deeper than the last. A prisoner thrust through the throat of the first would fall, say, twenty feet ; in the next the drop was deeper; the third was deeper still. In the last the victim plunged into the bottomless blackness of the mountain's heart.

There were many other dungeons, too, so safe, so chill, and so remote, a man might shriek himself to death within a few yards of sunshine and orange trees and flowers, and none know save God and the stone walls. There can be no manner of doubt that many so perished — men, women, and children, for Christophe's mercy was not.

I think the Black Emperor must have looked forward to a day when he would have to defend himself from his foes. The well he had constructed was deep and clear and freezing-cold, and fed by an inexhaustible spring. La Ferriére was his Tower of Babel; he built it to save him-self from the incoming flood of revolt which he feared; built it at an incredible waste of life and labour, and after all it never answered the purpose of its being.

It is magnificent. The price paid for it was thirty thousand lives.

To-day it is a cloud-hung ruin. The lizard keeps its gates, and the wind is alone in its vast emptinesses.

A ruin has always stamped upon it the traces of some human passion. This frowning helmet of La Ferriére bears the sign manual of the ferocity and merciless vigour of Christophe.

On the battlements you find yourself, as it were, on the roof of the world, looking upon the other side of the cloud-rack. One reaches it by a faint track curling up the mountain side, and in three hours you pass from the sundried breathless plain below to a region of wind, grey-black mists, and aching cold. It towers upon the last and highest precipice like some sinister monster of the elder world ready to launch itself forth upon the spreading lands below.

Seen from afar the Citadel reminds one of a Chitrali fort, one flat step of masonry above another, but nearer at hand it resolves itself into its true bold and menacing outlines. The conception of placing a fortress of such immense strength and size in such a position could only have come to a ruler who did not count cost in lives and labour. But the black Emperor was a man who knew his own mind and understood thoroughly the gentle art of tearing down the barriers of laziness behind which the negro entrenches himself at all times.

The materials for the whole huge pile of building, and the three hundred pieces of ordnance with which it was fortified, were dragged up those steep mountain scarps and cliffsides by human hands. Christophe employed the troops mercilessly in this labour, seconding them by levies of peasants raised as required. These poor wretches had no pay and no food; they lived as they could, while their terrible master forced them on to a fever of toil by methods which left little chance of resistance.

Neither sex nor age was spared; the royal works had to be carried on in spite of exhaustion or death. Whips of cowskin, mercilessly applied by the officers in command, drew forth almost incredible reserves of energy. The mortality was frightful, but Christophe had the whole of the populous north to draw upon, and he used up human lives unsparingly.

It took a whole regiment a whole day to drag up a 32-pounder. On another occasion the Emperor watched a long line of a hundred men hauling a cannon upwards to its mountain resting-place. Now and then they paused in their labour, and these frequent stoppages annoyed Christophe; he sent to ask the why and wherefore. The labourers returned for answer that the gun was over much for the strength of a hundred men, and prayed that another hundred men might be provided to help them.

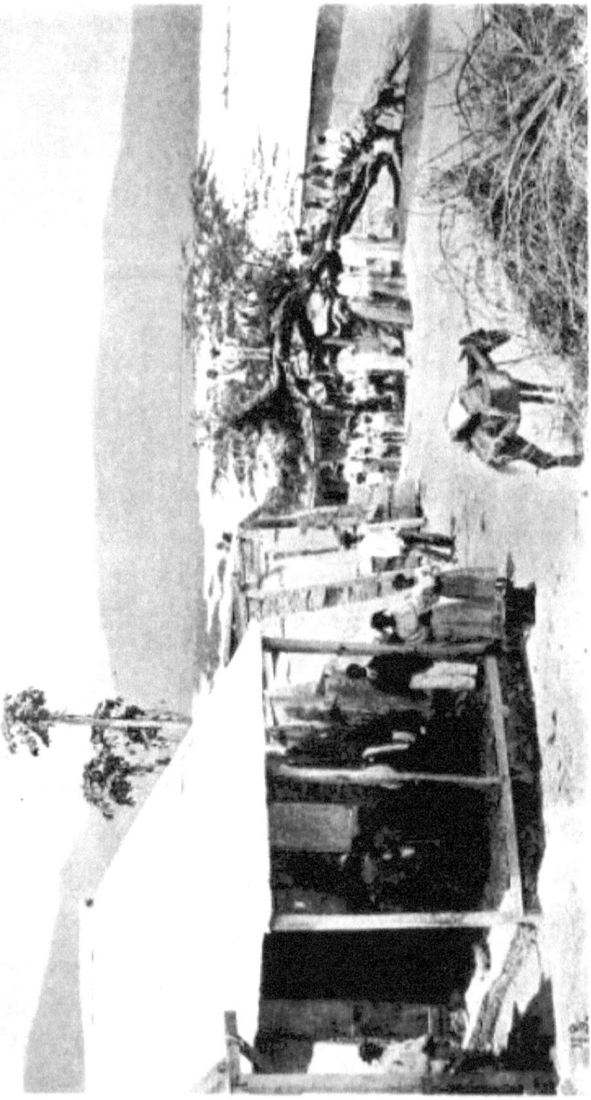

BEL-AIR.

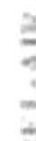

Christophe ordered them before him and talked softly with them, and at length told them to fall in and number off. He then directed every fourth man to fall out, and, calling up his guards, had them shot. When it was over, he informed the remaining seventy-five that he was but half-way through his lunch, and he would consider it a favour if they would run the gun up into place before he had finished.

The diminished band went back to work, but by the time Christophe's meal was over the cannon had made but little progress up the mountain side. When he arrived on the scene the seventy-five bore witness with one voice that the thing he required was, for so small a number, impossible.

Christophe laughed. "So it seems," he said, "but I have a remedy. Fall in."

They fell in, and numbered off as before.

"Every third man fall out. Guards, shoot these men."

The volley had scarcely died away and the last limb ceased to quiver, when Christophe gave his ultimatum.

"Now," he said to the frightened residue, "I will require every second man to fall out next time. The gun was too heavy for a hundred men, surely fifty will find it light."

They did. At any rate, they towed it up to the summit of La Ferriére, and in its appointed casemate it probably stands to this day. By such means the Citadel came to be the wonderful achievement it is.

On those towering heights it was painfully laid, stone on stone, by men and women driven to superhuman effort by the fear of unheard-of punishments. For Christophe was of an original turn of mind, and an epicure in torture. A man does not, I take it, know how he can work until he has real fear dogging him.

Christophe's agent in England (a prince, by the way, created under the new empire) boasted of his master's public works, "ravines filled up" and the like. He did not add the *modus operandi*; which was simple. If Christophe, in driving, came to a hollow place he caused a drum to be beaten. All within hearing were compelled to come to the spot on pain of death. The Emperor would point to the offending hole or valley — it mattered little which it was — and remarked that he would pass by that way again at such a time. That was all. When he returned, if the work did not suit his ideas or had not been completed, the drum sounded again, and on the people assembling he would choose out a casual half-dozen and have them shot then and there.

There seems to have been nothing to appeal to in this man's nature. Bravery, humility, all alike failed to touch him. He had no bowels of mercy. He was one day on the battlements with a youth, who, perhaps presuming on past favours, in some manner displeased him. The drop from those sheer walls is 2,000ft. to the plain below.

"You are, of course, about to die," said Christophe, " but I will be kind to you. You shall have a choice of deaths. Either you throw yourself over here or the soldiers shall shoot you."

The young man chose to fling himself into space. But by a miracle he fell amongst some trees or bushes on the cliff-side, and so escaped with a broken arm. He gathered himself up somehow, and presented himself again before the Emperor.

"Your bidding has been done, sire," he said.

"Yes, it has," remarked Christophe, "and I am very much interested to find that you survive. Oblige me by trying if you can do it again!"

These are the stories which cling round the name of Christophe. He was not a Haytian negro, but from one of the English islands near. For this reason, perhaps, one takes an unwholesome pride in the man, as possessed of a rare character and indomitable resolution, much in the same way as we are proud of the great pirate, Captain Kidd, another gentleman who had to do with Hayti, for his treasure is said to be hidden in the neighbouring island of Tortuga, which lies close to the coast and belongs to the Republic.

The Black Napoleon was a man of rapid rise. He entered the army, did some service in a tumult of revolution, then contrived a coup-d'etat, and he was master of the situation. By these few steps he raised himself to the head of events, and at once created an Empire out of the Northern Provinces.

Unlike the majority of his race, he possessed many of the qualities of a born ruler. He made himself immortal by his masterful vigour, which on the one side, it is true, degenerated into callous brutality, but on the other rose to that energising force of character that is said to have initiated a spirit of enterprise and industry in the north — a spirit that up to the present day differentiates his old kingdom from the rest of the Black Republic. On the whole, it can hardly be denied that he was somewhat of a kingly figure. And the manner of his death was in keeping with his life.

Towards the close he had an attack of paralysis, and as soon as he recovered sufficiently to give orders he had himself placed in a bath of rum and pepper, a remedy that somewhat restored him. Immediately after a revolution broke out against him at Cap Haytien, provoked by his merciless exactions of labour from the people. From the belvedere of his Palace of Sans-Souci he watched the rebels burning his fields of cane; he sent for his body-guard, and, as they defiled before him, he gave each man a dollar, and bade them go and fight against the rebels. Later, news was brought that the guard had deserted, and gone over to the enemy. He must have felt that the end of his power was come. He rose and bade farewell to his wife and family, and, going to his own chamber, blew out his brains.

As always happens in such cases, the servants and officers of the court looted the palace, but his wife and daughters managed to carry away his dead body with them to the Citadel on the mountain above. At times, they say, a grim shadow rises from the jungle grown tomb and wanders about the battlements, overlooking the plains that were once his own.

The climate of the Citadel up there among the clouds is full of rapid and bewildering changes. One moment the heat is tropical. Then you see far away a cloud ; it approaches, rearing up into the zenith, rushing at you like a regiment of cavalry in a wide swirl of black dust. The next moment it is belching in at all the embrasures, chilling you to the bone, and the climate becomes that of the outer Hebrides, During these sudden invasions the place gives you the concrete representation of all that is chaotic and ruinous and abysmal.

When the rain and the mist had passed over we went out again across the threshold. The sun was shining, and over the vista of potato-green plain and amethyst sea the cloud was gathering up its ragged skirts in flight.

As I left the tall warder was pessimistically picking over the remnants of my late repast, and he had warmed the fire into flickering life. Another heavy-breasted cloud had invested the frowning walls; beneath their shadow the men were crouching together in their dreary hut, and above them the dying fortress hung hooded.

11

Justice and the Status of the White Where He is Ruled by the Negro

In most countries where they put forward race distinctions a man is called Englishman, American, German — by the name of whatever nation may claim him. But in Hayti the point of complexion carries the day, and establishes your designation. If you do not happen to be of the regnant colour, you are a white, a *blanc* — the Haytian recognises no minor distinction among the lighter-hued foreigners. As you walk about the streets you catch, at the tags and tails of sentences, the labial "*blanc*," as the curious or antagonist negro delivers his criticism upon you, your probable station in life, your present business and your personal charms. For, above all things, the negro is extraordinarily inquisitive.

Jealousy of the foreigner is a very pronounced trait, from the Government down to the wharf-side loafer. His immigration is discouraged in every way. He may be said to have practically no rights

; he can own no property in land, and if he gets a concession from the Government he is likely to find himself, sooner or later, left in the lurch.

Yet it is not too much to say that the presence of the white element, small as it is, makes for good. Remove it, and the Republic would go sliding back into the depths of barbarism. This applies more especially to the representatives of foreign Powers accredited to the island. Time and again has Hayti, in the course of her hundred years of independence, owed the continuance of that independence to the kind offices of these gentlemen.

Occasionally she flounders diplomatically, and then it is that the white man's aid must be called in to adjust a difficulty beyond the powers of the black. A schedule of the cases where the diplomatic representatives of foreign nations have saved Hayti from the wrath and reprisals of some insulted Power would make an interesting document, and, to those who are not behind the scenes, a surprisingly lengthy one.

For all this, Haytian gratitude is not. Unless the *quid pro quo* be down in black and white, and, moreover, insisted upon, it quietly drops into oblivion and no more is heard of it.

Here is an instance when the diplomatic corps formed the buffer between Haytian maladroitness and foreign resentment. The 6th of December, 1897, was a day to be long remembered in Port-au-Prince, for on that morning the German Government sent in an ultimatum. It is unnecessary to enter at length into the origin of the dispute, suffice it to say that a German subject had been imprisoned, and his release, on the intervention of his Minister, refused. In the end the man was set at liberty through the good offices of the American representative. But Germany considered herself insulted. The Kaiser sent a telegram, followed up by two gun-boats, with orders to receive the indemnity demanded, and, in the event of a refusal to pay, they were instructed to shell the capital.

Port-au-Prince was in an uproar. The inhabitants fled to the hills, the families of many leading citizens were sent on board the ships that happened to be lying in the harbour. The rougher part of the populace boasted that on the first shot fired they would begin a massacre of every white man, woman, and child in the town. The Cabinet met at the palace of the President to discuss the situation. Meantime the minutes were flying, but the foreign representatives procured an extension of the time-limit given in the German ultimatum. The final hour fixed upon was one o'clock, on the stroke of which, as the German commander was careful to assure them, the first shell would

12

Justice and the Status of the White Where He is Ruled by the Negro

In most countries where they put forward race distinctions a man is called Englishman, American, German — by the name of whatever nation may claim him. But in Hayti the point of complexion carries the day, and establishes your designation. If you do not happen to be of the regnant colour, you are a white, a *blanc* — the Haytian recognises no minor distinction among the lighter-hued foreigners. As you walk about the streets you catch, at the tags and tails of sentences, the labial "*blanc,*" as the curious or antagonist negro delivers his criticism upon you, your probable station in life, your present business and your personal charms. For, above all things, the negro is extraordinarily inquisitive.

Jealousy of the foreigner is a very pronounced trait, from the Government down to the wharf-side loafer. His immigration is discouraged in every way. He may be said to have practically no rights

; he can own no property in land, and if he gets a concession from the Government he is likely to find himself, sooner or later, left in the lurch.

Yet it is not too much to say that the presence of the white element, small as it is, makes for good. Remove it, and the Republic would go sliding back into the depths of barbarism. This applies more especially to the representatives of foreign Powers accredited to the island. Time and again has Hayti, in the course of her hundred years of independence, owed the continuance of that independence to the kind offices of these gentlemen.

Occasionally she flounders diplomatically, and then it is that the white man's aid must be called in to adjust a difficulty beyond the powers of the black. A schedule of the cases where the diplomatic representatives of foreign nations have saved Hayti from the wrath and reprisals of some insulted Power would make an interesting document, and, to those who are not behind the scenes, a surprisingly lengthy one.

For all this, Haytian gratitude is not. Unless the *quid pro quo* be down in black and white, and, moreover, insisted upon, it quietly drops into oblivion and no more is heard of it.

Here is an instance when the diplomatic corps formed the buffer between Haytian maladroitness and foreign resentment. The 6th of December, 1897, was a day to be long remembered in Port-au-Prince, for on that morning the German Government sent in an ultimatum. It is unnecessary to enter at length into the origin of the dispute, suffice it to say that a German subject had been imprisoned, and his release, on the intervention of his Minister, refused. In the end the man was set at liberty through the good offices of the American representative. But Germany considered herself insulted. The Kaiser sent a telegram, followed up by two gun-boats, with orders to receive the indemnity demanded, and, in the event of a refusal to pay, they were instructed to shell the capital.

Port-au-Prince was in an uproar. The inhabitants fled to the hills, the families of many leading citizens were sent on board the ships that happened to be lying in the harbour. The rougher part of the populace boasted that on the first shot fired they would begin a massacre of every white man, woman, and child in the town. The Cabinet met at the palace of the President to discuss the situation. Meantime the minutes were flying, but the foreign representatives procured an extension of the time-limit given in the German ulti-matum. The final hour fixed upon was one o'clock, on the stroke of which, as the German commander was careful to assure them, the first shell would

13

Justice and the Status of the White Where He is Ruled by the Negro

In most countries where they put forward race distinctions a man is called Englishman, American, German — by the name of whatever nation may claim him. But in Hayti the point of complexion carries the day, and establishes your designation. If you do not happen to be of the regnant colour, you are a white, a *blanc* — the Haytian recognises no minor distinction among the lighter-hued foreigners. As you walk about the streets you catch, at the tags and tails of sentences, the labial "*blanc,*" as the curious or antagonist negro delivers his criticism upon you, your probable station in life, your present business and your personal charms. For, above all things, the negro is extraordinarily inquisitive.

Jealousy of the foreigner is a very pronounced trait, from the Government down to the wharf-side loafer. His immigration is discouraged in every way. He may be said to have practically no rights;

he can own no property in land, and if he gets a concession from the Government he is likely to find himself, sooner or later, left in the lurch.

Yet it is not too much to say that the presence of the white element, small as it is, makes for good. Remove it, and the Republic would go sliding back into the depths of barbarism. This applies more especially to the representatives of foreign Powers accredited to the island. Time and again has Hayti, in the course of her hundred years of independence, owed the continuance of that independence to the kind offices of these gentlemen.

Occasionally she flounders diplomatically, and then it is that the white man's aid must be called in to adjust a difficulty beyond the powers of the black. A schedule of the cases where the diplomatic representatives of foreign nations have saved Hayti from the wrath and reprisals of some insulted Power would make an interesting document, and, to those who are not behind the scenes, a surprisingly lengthy one.

Here is an instance when the diplomatic corps formed the buffer between Haytian maladroitness and foreign resentment. The 6th of December, 1897, was a day to be long remembered in Port-au-Prince, for on that morning the German Government sent in an ultimatum. It is unnecessary to enter at length into the origin of the dispute, suffice it to say that a German subject had been imprisoned, and his release, on the intervention of his Minister, refused. In the end the man was set at liberty through the good offices of the American representative. But Germany considered herself insulted. The Kaiser sent a telegram, followed up by two gun-boats, with orders to receive the indemnity demanded, and, in the event of a refusal to pay, they were instructed to shell the capital.

Port-au-Prince was in an uproar. The inhabitants fled to the hills, the families of many leading citizens were sent on board the ships that happened to be lying in the harbour. The rougher part of the populace boasted that on the first shot fired they would begin a massacre of every white man, woman, and child in the town. The Cabinet met at the palace of the President to discuss the situation. Meantime the minutes were flying, but the foreign representatives procured an extension of the time-limit given in the German ultimatum. The final hour fixed upon was one o'clock, on the stroke of which, as the German commander was careful to assure them, the first shell would

For all this, Haytian gratitude is not. Unless the *quid pro quo* be down in black and white, and, moreover, insisted upon, it quietly drops into oblivion and no more is heard of it.

Here is an instance when the diplomatic corps formed the buffer between Haytian maladroitness and foreign resentment. The 6th of December, 1897, was a day to be long remembered in Port-au-Prince, for on that morning the German Government sent in an ultimatum. It is unnecessary to enter at length into the origin of the dispute, suffice it to say that a German subject had been imprisoned, and his release, on the intervention of his Minister, refused. In the end the man was set at liberty through the good offices of the American representative. But Germany considered herself insulted. The Kaiser sent a telegram, followed up by two gun-boats, with orders to receive the indemnity demanded, and, in the event of a refusal to pay, they were instructed to shell the capital.

Port-au-Prince was in an uproar. The inhabitants fled to the
hills, the families of many leading citizens were sent on board the

ships that happened to be lying in the harbour. The rougher part of the populace boasted that on the first shot fired they would begin a massacre of every white man, woman, and child in the town. The Cabinet met at the palace of the President to discuss the situation. Meantime the minutes were flying, but the foreign representatives procured an extension of the time-limit given in the German ultimatum. The final hour fixed upon was one o'clock, on the stroke of which, as the German commander was careful to assure them, the first shell would be dropped upon the roof of the palace unless a white flag, the signal of compliance, should be hoisted there.

The Cabinet were on the horns of a dilemma; they did not know how the populace would take surrender. For the Haytians at large have no idea of their position in the catalogue of the nations, being fully convinced that they could engage on equal terms with any one of them. Without the advice and mediation of the foreign delegates, there can be little doubt that the time-limit would have expired and that Hayti must in consequence have felt the weight of Germany's hand, even if the wild anarchy that would inevitably have broken out had not marked the end of her century of independence.

And the German affair is only one of many. Thanks, then, to events such as these, while he is, with rare exceptions, disliked and distrusted, the average foreigner has earned at least the toleration which is invariably accorded to usefulness. In this connection the visit of the German warships had one good effect. It brought home to the Haytian in the street, the knowledge that white is a colour worthy of respect. For a foreign gun- boat in Port-au-Prince bay is worth more as a deterrent than a navy at Port Royal. The black man must see to understand.

As to the personal safety of the foreigner, he has under the present regime little cause for complaint. Of course it is fatally easy, if you are not known, to get into trouble, and once in you will find it an uncommonly hard matter to get out again.

On many occasions during my stay in Port-au-Prince I crossed the Champ-de-Mars late at night. A better place to rob a man you could not find in the two hemispheres. It is lonely, it is dark, its lamps are broken, it is honeycombed with treacherous holes and ditches, whence the bull-frogs croak ceaselessly. It would not be wise to cross it in the small hours, were it situated in Venezuela, where the early pedestrian is apt to find such objects as unidentified fingers on the public paths — three were found in Carracas not a month ago — but here beyond the ubiquitous, cent-desiring soldier, you are never molested. At least, that was my experience.

This is a surprising condition of affairs when you consider the state of Hayti. It is another of those violent contrasts in which this country is so rich. Her people, whatever may be their other faults, have not that knife-in-your-back instinct which permeates so many of the Spanish-American Republics.

And now, having dealt with the safety of the white man from the attacks of the lawless, let us see how he is likely to fare if he chances to be attacked by the law.

The *blanc* is not infrequently thrown into prison on frivolous charges, and when one takes into account the chances of maltreatment on arrest, and the horribly insanitary condition of the prisons, this in itself constitutes a grave danger. Further, his evidence in the courts does not, under any circumstances, hold good against counter-evidence offered by a Haytian. Whatever the rights of the case may be, it is a foregone conclusion that the Juge de Paix will decide in favour of his own countryman.

Outside the Legations, the Consulates, and the chief mercantile houses, the white man in Hayti cannot be called a particularly fine example of the aristocracy of colour. Five men out of six have had chameleon careers, and have been fired at last by the rigour of stark necessity into their present berths. The greater number of them are, of course, Germans. At the close of the last century it was estimated that the white population of Hayti reckoned 46,000 souls; to-day you might knock off the last two ciphers.

And with the disappearance of the white colonists prosperity fled from the land. Government policy, as has been said, is directed towards keeping out the foreigner. The result is that the immense natural resources of the country remain entirely undeveloped. The white man has of necessity to be very circumspect in his dealings with the Haytian. He lives and trades in the Republic under protest, as it were, against a regime that is always antagonistic, and ready to hamper his efforts whenever opportunity offers.

As far as the towns are concerned, then, the white man, if he can keep clear of the entanglements of the law, will not, save in unusual cases, be molested. A revolution, of course, alters the aspect of things, promiscuous shooting goes on, and underlying dislike of the outlander comes to the surface. But even when things are taking their normal course, if he happens to be unfortunate enough to come within the grasp of the law, the White, under the present Government, has no rights the Black need respect save those which can be enforced by his diplomatic representative, which means by the brute power of his nation.

In all the principal coast towns there exists a little nucleus of white men, who form the core of the virile part of the community, and who, if they make their money out of the country, bring much into it. Their daily life is monotonous enough. Take, by way of example, the routine at the Cape. A man is up with the sun or before it, and arrives at his office early. Breakfast is taken at noon, after which he returns to work. About four he adjourns as one man to the local club, and there he stays till seven, playing billiards or dominoes, or sitting on the wooden piazza that overlooks the ragged weed-grown marsh. After that he goes home to dinner and bed. And to-morrow he travels the same old round. So runs life for the foreigner in Hayti.

If you are a white man, then don't go to law in Hayti. Bribery is not unknown, but it is nearly always far cheaper to submit to injustice than to try conclusions in a law court. For you cannot bribe away, even if you wished to, the self-evident fact of race, and your opponent usually happens to be of the ruling colour.

The basis of the law is the Code Napoleon, modified to Haytian necessities, and altered in lesser particulars from time to time. The judicial machinery of the courts, from the Court of Cassation downwards, is modelled upon the French system. The judges are black, for any admixture of blood is regarded with strong disfavour, and even mulattoes are rigorously excluded from positions and authority. The better class do not seek the office, and judges, oddly enough, are rarely drawn from the grades of the legal profession.

The President has the right of nomination, and he and his party put forward any person they please, for a judge's most prominent recommendation is his usefulness as a partisan or supporter. The actual salary is small, but the appointment can be and is so handled as to prove highly remunerative.

It is a fact of common knowledge that cases are .systematically prejudged; now and then a politician intervenes quietly for purposes of his own; he gives a hint to the bench, and the verdict is arranged before the litigants set foot in court. Curious impediments are thrown in the way of justice, and grotesque excuses have been given for the non-fulfilment of ordinary legal forms.

In this connection a story may be told which has a

moral, but no end. In a certain town there is a firm whom we will call Da Costa and Co. Some years ago they made an arrangement with a Haytian to buy for them certain materials required in their business.

To carry out his side of the contract, and for the express purpose of procuring the various articles in demand, the Haytian went to Europe, taking with him a large advance of some thousands from the company. He visited most of the Continental cities, spending a long interval at the Mecca of Haytians — Paris, and by the end of a year or so returned home empty-handed. He had no money left, nor had he any supplies to show.

Da Costa and Co naturally objected to the complete disappearance of their money, and took the matter into court, and there it still remains. The evidence was so clear that a record was broken and judgment given for the plaintiffs. But, having done this, the judges manifestly thought they had done enough. They had given a verdict in favour of a firm of foreigners, and it was now necessary to remove the stain of so doing from their characters.

The course they adopted was of a simplicity akin to genius — they refused to execute the judgment. On the occasion of Messrs. Da Costa's last appeal, the excuse was beautifully consistent with Haytian traditions. The court (and it was not an inferior court, quite the opposite) replied that they had at the moment no money to buy the necessary stamped paper to execute the judgment, and Messrs. Da Costa must wait until they had!

To show the converse side of the shield of Republican justice — at this moment there is more than one foreigner in gaol for the crime of owing a dollar or some similar small sum to a Haytian.

Those who gain their cases may safely be divided into three classes. First, the black, whose opponent is white, wholly or partially; secondly, as among themselves, the man with the biggest purse and pull ; and, lastly, in the lower classes, the man who has the luck. Occasionally extraneous influences are brought to bear. As in the old Roman days, the sword thrown into the balance brings down the scales of justice with a run.

Recently a Haytian merchant sued the active Chief of Police for debt. On the day the case was called the Chief of Police made up a snug little escort of his men, and, to give due weight to the proceedings, served out a few rounds of ammunition, and marched them in a body up to the court. Three black judges were on the bench ready to try the case — two of them forestalled trouble by recollecting pressing engagements elsewhere, and the third sought cover. The case was adjourned for a fortnight.

On the day fixed for the second hearing the Chief of Police played trumps again, the judges departed at the double and there was no quorum.

Upon this the Chief Justice wrote to the defendant. He begged him to bear in mind his duties as a citizen, and to present himself before the Civil Tribune in a costume and manner conforming to the laws of his country.

For answer, upon the appointed day the Chief doubled his escort, dressed himself in full uniform, served out some extra boxes of ammunition for his men to carry, and rode his horse into the court. The case was postponed, and postponed it remains at the hour of writing. It is reported that political animus was here the wheel within the wheel.

In criminal cases the courts move slowly about their business. The law of habeas corpus is a dead letter. A man may lie in prison awaiting trial for no small period of time. There is to-day a prisoner in the jail at Port-auPrince. He has been there for many years, and no record of his offence remains ; the why and the wherefore have been long forgotten. Only the man himself is extant, still undergoing the punishment of his lost crime.

There is in the constitution a law abolishing the penalty of death for political misdemeanours, but it was consistently ignored by every President, without exception, who has held power in the island, until General Sam, who is now at the head of the Government, came into office. To his credit be it said that he usually sends his political enemies to prison instead of shooting them out of hand against the crumbling arsenal wall, after the immortal principles of his predecessors Salomon and Hippolyte. But I could name one gentleman at least who, if he succeeds to the Presidential chair, which is quite on the cards, will revive the good old customs of the past.

In spite, however, of the very general corruption and deliberate miscarriage of justice, the Court of Cassation has of late taken up an attitude which approximates more nearly to the universal idea of equity, and has decided some cases upon their own merits and not upon those of the litigants.

Judicial procedure is in certain instances not untouched by humour. A Haytian owed a trader twenty-eight dollars. A judgment requiring the Haytian to pay four dollars a week into court was given, and the trader agreed to send a messenger every week to the magistrate for the money. In due time he sent for the first instalment, and was informed that the Haytian had not paid up, but that he should be thrown into prison for his failure.-

Three weeks passed with the same result. One morning the Haytian came to the trader's store. He was, he said, a poor man, much married, a man to whom therefore expense came. What good, he asked, would accrue to the trader if he, the poor man, was thrown into prison? Let the trader forgive him his debt, and earn thereby untold rewards in a future state.

After some talk the trader gave him a letter of remission, which he went oft to present to the magistrate. The affair was settled, but the Haytian was struck by the bad grace with which the magistrate dismissed him, and he forthwith returned to the trader and asked him if he had received the eight dollars already paid into court. The trader looked surprised, and said he had received nothing.

"Then, since you have remitted the debt, that eight dollars is mine," said the Haytian.

Accordingly he went off to the court to present his claim. The magistrate at once committed him to prison. A consul who had heard the story asked the magistrate what the Haytian was sent to prison for.

"For contempt of court," was the reply.

14

The Haytian Press

If I were condemned to write down the names of all the newspapers of Hayti, past and present, I should have to spend a considerable time upon the task. The reason of their multiplicity is not on account of any great demand for news in the Black Republic, but because from a number of causes the journals of the daily press are apt to be short-lived.

Whenever there is a revolution each party, each powerful leader, must perforce have an organ through which he may address the public generally and the inhabitants of Port-au-Prince in particular. So each political commotion brings in its train a crop of newspapers, proclamations, pamphlets — call them what you will — whose average length of life is limited to half-a-dozen issues.

Moreover, a paper which starts its career in print as "The Evening News of Hayti " may pass through various re-incarnations; so that when "The Evening News" happens to be suppressed on a Saturday, it makes its reappearance on Monday under the alias of (say) "The Mirror of the World;" after being once more put down it turns up shortly as "The Thunderer of the Republic."

These journals have a humour of their own for the European reader. They are conducted by Haytian journalists whose styles appear to lend themselves to a rather bombastic tone, and whose grasp upon foreign affairs is superlatively French.

Although there appears to be some competition among the newspapers, circulation is counted by tens instead of by thousands, and the means by which the chief Republican organs exist are drawn from the subsidies granted to them by the State. This system naturally militates against a free and fearless press. In any case, it must be difficult to preserve freedom of utterance when, at the first symptom of independence, the enterprising editor is dragged off to prison. Ten years ago the Haytian press was in a more healthy condition than it is to-day. At that time grievances were published, brutal arrests condemned, and the evils of the country, even cannibalism and snake-worship, were occasionally dealt with. The greatest newspaper of those days was run by the Consul-General of the rival black Republic of Liberia.

At the present time Port-au-Prince possesses two papers, "Le Soir" and "Le Nouvelliste," whose views upon local questions are absolutely colourless. In form they are like a single page of "The St. James's Gazette," but the paper upon which they appear has vast margins. Their contents include telegrams from French sources, an article by a leading Haytian, and a patchwork of utterly unimportant local news. When they find themselves short of copy they print a eulogy of the President of Hayti, or of the editor of the paper.

In the front column of one of these papers, directly under the head of "Foreign Telegrams," appeared the following interesting announcement:

"M. Salmon has removed for M. C. Rigaud four corns and an ingrowing nail without pain or effusion of blood. He was very satisfied with the manner in which Pedicure Salmon operated.

To-morrow will be the turn of D. Narcisse and on Friday that of the Editor of this paper." — " Le Peuple."

Another gem is the following: —

"EXTRAORDINARY FACT. — One of the sons of Dr. Maitre Bonaventure, the Port doctor, was a victim last night of an attempted assassination accomplished under circumstances which have yet to be explained. Being in his bed alone in the house, and all the means of ingress absolutely closed, he received several blows from a poignard! We have ourselves heard certain persons seriously lay this mysterious crime to the charge of Satan! We believe that Justice has accepted this interpretation with a wise reserve. We await further revelations with expectation." — "La Revue Expres."

The price of newspapers ranges from five centimes to half a dollar. I understand that their circulation occasionally attains four figures, but I believe three would be nearer the mark.

During the earlier part of the Boer War I suffered considerably at the hands of the Haytian press. Their rendering of events, being drawn from the French point of view, was alarmist.

Under date 13th December, General "Forestier" includes in his despatch from the Cape the following news of General Methuen: — "The Boers being perfectly entrenched this morning in their position, I retired in good order, and up to the present I am safe."

We have heard a great deal lately of the French press campaign against us. Hayti lies, as everyone knows, 4,000 miles distant from France, yet one of these Haytian papers, which I have described above, published an article last December, some extracts from which are worth quoting.

Napoleon, risen from his tomb at the Invalides, addresses his old soldiers: "The English, the eternal enemy who conquered you — for in conquering me she conquered you — the English of Trafalgar and of Waterloo, recoil before the energy of a little people of Africa. The mercenaries of the Old Queen draw back, and are broken ; the officers fall to save the honour of the flag that these mercenaries have not the heart to defend; Albion fights no longer , . . Albion dies . . . And thou, France, thou wilt look on and thou wilt not budge!

"What then is the blood that flows in thy veins? Hast thou forgotten that I fought for twenty years to deliver thee from her commercial yoke? That I conquered at Jena, at Austerlitz, at Eylau, to chastise, not the Prussian, not the Russian, not the Austrian, but to destroy the English? Hast thou forgotten that thy last glory, the purest of all, that which lit up the end of the century with a ray of greatness and hope, the glory of Marchand and of his band of heroes, has been torn from thee by this race of shopkeepers?

"And if thou hast not forgotten these sorrows, why dost thou delay to avenge them?

"Already at Boulogne I had gathered an army. . . . Under their eyes, notwithstanding their cruisers, I was preparing to invade them. In a few days I should have thrown 100,000 men into their island. To-day 20,000 would suffice to muzzle them. Their vessels are at the end of the earth; thine are here.

"They will escort thy transports, which, in less than twenty-four hours, will disembark on this accursed island the sons of my old Grenadiers! France, to arms ! It is not to a conquest that I invite you, it is to give a vital blow to these insolents! Republic, remember Hoche! France, bethink thee of Bonaparte!" On coming to an end of these inspired words, the shade disappeared.

At times the editors of the Haytian papers have singular difficulties to contend with. One organ announced its desire to buy new forms, but said it must postpone the purchase until the newsagents who retailed its copies paid some of their debts on account.

To wind up, I will give you some war correspondence in the Haytian style. The following were produced during the Dominican War or one or other of the many revolutions: —

"The two armies met; after a terrible battle lasting two hours, which cost the life of a man, our troops carried the enemy's camp by assault."

Here again: —

"To-day, rising to the height of the sublime sentiment of independence, the citizens of Valliere shouted the cry of indissoluble fraternity ! The enemy launched against us the whole of their forces ; the lesson has been a terrible one; three drums, a trumpet, and various other objects remained in the hands of the troops of the Government. Honour to the Generals A — , B — , C — , D — , E— , &c."

And here is an address from a General to his soldiers: —

"Soldiers! — I promised to conduct you to victory, and your first enterprises have been fruitful 1 Put your trust then in the wisdom and the experience with which I direct your steps. Soon, the God of Armies blessing our arms, complete triumph will crown our efforts, for we defend a just cause, a holy cause — that of public liberty!"

A week later this patriot emptied the Treasury, sold his party to the enemy, tried during a night disturbance to overthrow the President, and fled to Europe.

To conclude, I give an advertisement of a different kind.

"The undersigned wishes to bring to the notice of the public the fact that since his return from Panama, now almost six years ago, he has not meddled with any sums in gold or silver belonging to an)' person whatsoever. He trusts that having said this an impartial public will meditate on the announcement." — " Le Peuple." (Advt.)

15

The Haytian People As I Knew Them

THEY are kindly. They are hospitable. They are goodhearted. They are a song-loving and a cheerful people.

They are ignorant. They are lazy. They are leavened with the horrors of serpent-worship, and a certain, though I think a diminishing, proportion of them consent (to say the least of it) to human sacrifice.

That is the good and bad of the Black Republic of the West. In their defence, let it be said that they are brutally misgoverned. And by reason of the secret influence of the Papalois their worst faults and superstitions are kept alive and pandered to. Yet, in spite of all these drawbacks, I have never during all my travels in the wild districts asked for a drink of water in vain. Small farmers, or those who in any other country would answer to such a description, men who had never seen me before, dwelling in poor, hump-backed huts have given me a mattress and what meagre food they had, without ever expecting repayment, and indeed they were insulted if I offered it.

It is a country of gigantic contrasts, of no sort of mediocrity. The Haytian is either one thing or the other, a sort of Man in the Moon, entirely lacking in mental atmosphere, capable of passing instantaneously from intensest light to blackest shadow, from kindly hospitality to hopeless cruelty.

The so-called wild people of the interior are utterly maligned. You may chance, as I did, to run up against some priest-dominated Vaudoux worshipper who will try to poison you by means of some obscure and potent drug. You may witness orgies and sacrifices, if you can contrive to be present and are willing to take the risk. They go on all the year round, although with greater license at certain periods. If you offend the authorities in any outof-the-way place, yours may not be a very enviable fate, for when the negro finds a white man in his power the result, as far as the white man is concerned, becomes precisely what the negro's whim may make it.

Yet the rural Haytian is all that I have said, for the foreigner who gets into trouble amongst them has to deal, not with them, but with the local authority — that is, the General de la Place. He is a black endowed with arbitrary powers, and, consequently, is often of swollen pretensions.

He rules precisely as rules the biggest boy at school; he deals out a rough and ready justice that would be humorous were it not terrific. He awards the penalty of death with the same lightness of heart that a large boy bestows on a smaller the harmless and necessary kick. Yet, to judge broadly from effects, this off-hand system excellently suits the character of the people.

In the towns matters are rather different. The townloafer is not deserving of much praise. The wharfside nigger steals with as much frequency as he eats; that is, he seeks the chance all the day and most of the night. When working on a lighter, his favourite game is to drop a barrel overboard, sink it, and fish it up again in the small hours. He hangs about ships in his boat, picking up every trifle he can lay hands on.

ON A JOURNEY.

Occasionally someone in authority breaks up his foolish jackdaw's hoard, he is arrested and clubbed by the police, taken away to the prison where no food is, and there chained to an iron bar. It does him no good. He is a thief of thieves, and will go on stealing until he is dead, and then probably some of his friends will come along and steal the boots from the corpse. Above these petty offenders are the great Generals, who steal the soldiers' pay; and, still higher, the Government, who steal promiscuously from all and everywhere.

As to the negro's position in the Government, there are in the Cabinet some capable men of African race, but sandwiched in amongst them are others who are mere caricatures — men whose deserved place, I really do not think I am unjust or unfair in saying, ought to be rather the stoke-hole of a steamer. One of the strongest tendencies in the Republic of to-day is the desire to keep the coloured, as opposed to the black, man from office and emolument. There is a rooted jealousy between the two classes, to which is added race-hatred.

If you look into Haytian history you will find cropping up throughout its pages the record of these fierce and sanguinary struggles; you will find the coloured element dwindling and continually growing smaller and less powerful. The personnel of the present Government is black enough to delight the heart of the most advanced negro-phile. President Sam is of the ultra-negro type, and all the higher posts around him are filled with men of his own race. "Hayti for the Haytians," that war-cry of the people of the Republic, means really Hayti for the negro — no mulatto need apply.

The people as a whole will rarely consent to vote for a mulatto, whilst when a negro enters the arena the result is a foregone conclusion. It is an every-day fact that the masses, who would individually poison a white man for a fancied slight, or would resent justice at the hands of a mulatto, submit contentedly to tyrannical oppression from one of their own colour! In the same way a regiment will cheerfully watch one of their comrades being clubbed into oblivion if the orders emanate from a negro officer, whereas they would mutiny were a mulatto in command to exercise a like right. In this brotherhood of colour lies the power of the Papaloi.

One of the points that strike you most is that Hayti is essentially a country of extremes and contrasts. Logic is always at fault. A Haytian's honesty is like a Haytian's mind; it is apt to surprise you round odd corners.

TYPICAL PEASANTRY.

For example: hundreds of thousands of Haytian dollars pass annually along the lonely track, which is called by courtesy a high road, between Jacmel and Port au-Prince. The men who bear them are low-class Haytians — ragged, uncouth, uneducated, wild, and untutored. Yet, in spite of the temptations of poverty, only once have the dollars failed to arrive.

This strange blend breeds theory. It is advanced that the courier does not steal because he has no use for the money, because his idea of wealth takes the form of fightingcocks, and surplus roosters are not his necessity. I have heard it said that ten dollars would tempt his cupidity, whereas ten thousand would awe him into immaculate honesty.

But over and above it all you may safely put it down that within certain set bounds the courier's honesty burns in a clear flame. To go back to the story of the one exception who broke the rule. He was a poor man, as all couriers are, and he was engaged to ride across from Jacmel to Port-au-Prince. Before he started certain other men came to him and put the theft into his mind. Somewhere on the road over the mountain he was to transfer the thirty thousand dollars to them, then they would clear off. To induce the courier to do this they offered him — what? Fifty dollars of the whole amount! His pay would have been about ten, so thus for forty dollars our courier fell from his high estate.

The story has a pathetic note in it, especially as the unfortunate man disappeared into prison and was heard of no more. During the last thirty years uncounted couriers have made the desolate journey by the lonely riverside track and over the mountain passes, each with his load of wealth, and the above is the only instance known of the betrayal of trust. A fine record.

As to these fellows, to trust them gives them the staff of self-respect. Yesterday the courier was a wandering nigger, a common bad-egg citizen of Hayti; to-day he is a man entrusted with thirty thousand dollars. He is not the same. From the chrysalis of obscurity he has become a butterfly in the fierce light of trust. He lives for the moment, to-morrow he will be nothing again. Never mind. For the moment he finds honesty to hang with the gourds and the money-bags upon his saddlebow, yet he is probably a serpent-worshipper.

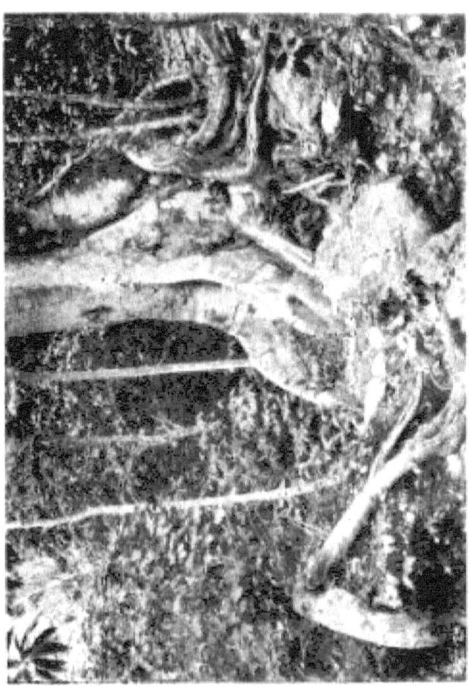

His self-respect, unlike the self-respect of a white, is not intrinsic; no man, indeed, has less. It is from outside that he gains it, and it consolidates him, stiffens him, changes him from a bad loafer into a good servant. He girds on a cutlass and sets forth singing a rude song, and he sings and smokes, fords rivers and climbs mountains for many hours, a Man. Once the strain is over, alas, he is apt to sink back into what he was before.

A courier who had brought thirty thousand dollars from Jacmel across the passes made them over intact to their consignee, and when leaving his office stole thirty cents and a penknife! The thirty thousand dollars were confided to his care, the thirty cents were a prey to his enterprise.

You must not forget that the negro has been for a century in touch with white men on the coast : in the interior he rarely sees a white face. Now, while on the coast I hold him to be often a very objectionable person, in the interior I have accepted the hospitality of his roof and lived with him, and, apart from his natural laziness and his inclination towards snake-worship, have found him a simple and unobtrusive being. Yet, the moment he prospers his good points fall away from him; he loses his perspective.

And here you come to the question of how far the Haytian negro has advanced from his initial stage of savagery. The huts in which he lives in the interior are the same as those in which his forefathers used to hve beside the Congo. He dresses Httle, but after the age of puberty rarely goes quite naked. He has few ambitions. His chief desire is to be let alone. Moreover, he firmly believes that if any white nation were to take over Hayti he would again become a slave.

The negro, then, in Hayti mostly turns his energies into one of three channels. He either helps to govern the country, is in Government service, or does odd jobs for a living. Otherwise he lives behind the big scarred, purple mountains, trusting to the soil to supply his wants, and dreaming away his life in a land where it is always afternoon.

Nine-tenths of the population of Hayti are negroes, and they form an ever-growing class. The tendency all over the country is to breed back to the African type. It is a curious fact that the negro hates the half-breed, the mulatto, considerably more than he hates the white man; but the negress, when she cannot get them white, prefers her admirers yellow, nor does this predilection on her part tend to lessen the loathing the man of mixed blood inspires in the breast of the black.

Although Hayti is by no means large, yet you find in different parts of the island almost separate races, dissimilar in build and features, and speaking distinguishable variants of Creole French. In the west and around the capital you have the descendants of the Mandingo tribes; in the Tiburon peninsula the Congo negro predominates. There are, of course, representatives of many other African races, and each of these has had some influence in modifying the dialect and mode of life in the particular part of the Republic which fortune may have made his headquarters.

In travelling through the country one is struck by the sorts, sizes, and shades to be met with. Black has variations of its own. There is the polished, jet-black skin and the dull, sooty complexion, while a fine mahogany black-brown often accompanies an upstanding figure and a pleasant face. As in Africa itself, so here one finds the black man fashioned on widely different patterns. Yet I have heard white men say that the power to distinguish one black face from another is the result of time and training, — that to the unaccustomed eye all really dark persons look much alike!

In a book of Haytian proverbs a story is told which possesses at least the seasoning of truth that is essential to artistic success in caricature. A white man, a mulatto, and a negro were one day summoned into the presence of their Maker, and each was asked what it was in the world that he most desired. The white man was prompt, he knew his own mind. He wanted knowledge. The mulatto desired beautiful women. But at first the negro had no answer to the question. After some sheepish evasions he pleaded that he had been brought there by the mulatto, and that if he really was to be given that which he most wanted he would like a piece of gold lace 1 After seeing a Haytian review you are inclined to credit the tale.

Hayti is rich in proverbs, most of which turn on the colour question. They are, of course, in the Creole dialect, and many are at once humorous and mordant, but they do not bear translating as a rule, for a large number deal with conditions of life that are local. Here is one, however, which has a general significance. "Wood is wood, but maple is not mahogany."

The greater part of the trade of the interior is in the hands of itinerant Syrian pedlars, of whom there are many thousands in Hayti. It is strange to find them in these Western islands. They are a race unspeakable, living ten in a room, consummate cheats; they are usurers and parasites sucking the blood from the country and in no way enriching their adopted land in return.

The Haytians do not like them, and legislate against their immigration, yet they are there in numbers. You meet them in the country districts, dirty, under-sized, well-featured people, followed by a boy carrying their box of goods. For a long time the Haytians regarded this comparatively fair-skinned race as white men, but they have learned that the Syrian will do anything for a five-cent piece. I have seen them take part in a Vaudoux sacrifice evidently belonging to the initiated.

The Haytian rarely marries; not because he does not wish to do so— indeed, it is considered a highly distinguished thing to be married — but because marriage by the rites of the Roman Catholic Church, which is supposed to be the religion of the State, costs about a hundred dollars, a prohibitive sum for the lower classes who favour the looser and less binding tie, which seems to serve them very well.

Family life with them appears to run on smooth lines. You rarely hear of a negress "changing" her husband, and the negro, owing to the predominant number of the opposite sex, indulges himself in as many wives as he can afford. I came across one man, who, like Priam, was the father of fifty, only the Haytian's brood was mixed, and not, as were the Trojan king's, all sons.

Every influential negro — this statement holds true of the wild rural districts, at any rate — is a polygamist. The number of his wives may range from two to fourteen — this last being the largest which came under my personal notice. If he has money enough he probably marries one of them, and the lady thus favoured will be thereafter the chief of his harem. Of course, these peculiar circumstances of life are not conducive to morality.

In fact, the rural Haytian blacks have no sense of morality in our meaning of the term. Wives are to the negro a source of wealth. They work for him, while he, with constitutional and ineradicable laziness, sits in the shade of his largest hut, and smokes a pipe with a red clay bowl all day long. Meantime his women and young children work. They will walk miles across a lonely and, during the rainy seasons, almost impassable country, carrying heavy loads upon their heads to the most favourable market. I say advisedly the young children, for directly the young buck becomes of an age to understand the dignity of his sex, he joins his father in lolling away the days, and works no more thenceforward for ever. If the patriarch deigns to go to market, he goes mounted on a small donkey, while his wives do the journey afoot.

And now to turn to their pleasures. They dance. In the capital, as in the country, it is their passion. Never are they too tired, never can a dance go on too long. The dances themselves are direct importations from the West Coast, and cannot be described as either graceful or in any degree beautiful. Their chief characteristic can be readily guessed at, considering that the performers are of the negro race. As you are riding through the country at night it is quite a common occurrence to come upon one of these dances going on within the stockade of old wood which surrounds each group of huts. A drum is always in the orchestra, and the sound of tom-toms is never absent.

You see the scene painted like a picture in red upon the blackness of the night. Fires throw up great wings of smoke, flaming lamps set in iron sockets and a torch or two light up the scene. The screams and the writhing contortions of the dancers, the ring of fire, the humpbacked huts throwing their monstrous shadows far beyond the circle of red light, the darkness of the listening forest — you have a scene which you are never likely to forget.

At other times, riding through the woodlands in the freshness of the morning or the evening, you see a solitary dancer posturing away grotesquely under a tree in some green nook.

The Bamboula, the Martinique, the Vaudoux are a few of the dance names. Sometimes these gatherings centre round a professional, who, clothed in a dress of barbaric colour, performs on a dais, and any man who likes may offer himself as her partner. It is common enough for a negress, who has walked twenty or perhaps many more miles since dawn, to spend the hours of darkness dancing monotonously until day comes to change the tints of the landscape.

In the capital there are four or five dances in progress every night. They are attended by all the lower classes; soldiers, boatmen, police, coffee-workers — that is, porters who carry bags of coffee for lading.

As for the upper ten in the towns you frequently see a stalwart Haytian followed by one, or it may be several boys (I fancy it is *chic* to employ many), the first carrying his walking-stick, another a newly-purchased packet of cigarettes, and so on, for to carry a parcel an inch long would bring a lasting stigma upon his pretension to fashion.

Fashion in Hayti, as elsewhere, is all-powerful. In its name the negro cheerfully endures many a weariness of the flesh. Fashion compels its votaries to a reign of black frock-coats in a tropical climate. Fashion it is, again, which decides that the "only wear" of the Haytian army on high days and holidays must be a uniform of cloth about a quarter of an inch in thickness. Fashion drives every man to wish to become a General, even though the State gives him no substantial means of supporting the position, and, as is the case in every country under the sun, rank brings its own expenses.

Among the richer classes there is a good deal of social life. Balls frequently take place, and are well attended, for Haytians high and low love dancing. From what I saw, however, I gathered that domestic bliss was more commonly to be found in the homes of the poorer peasantry than among the well-to-do of the towns. As soon as a man can afford to punctuate his day freely with "rhums" beseems to see no special reason for restraint, and this reacts not a little upon his family relations.

Marriage is the privilege of the wealthier part of the community, although only a proportion avail themselves of it. This is an omission upon which the local Mrs. Grundy looks with a lenient eye. And as by Haytian law the children of these looser unions are regarded as legitimate, the parents lack the strongest inducement to legalise their ties.

The Haytian politician forms a distinct section of the community, and cannot be dismissed with only a passing mention.

Take Paris, cut its comb, reduce and minimise it in almost all directions, material as well as intellectual, let it go to rack and ruin for a century, turn its whites into blacks and its blacks into whites, the temperate sky above it into tropical, scorching blue, and you would have some presentment of Port-au-Prince. Haytian life bears stamped upon it the likeness of France, and no individual shows it more palpably than the politician.

He is in many ways a highly superior specimen of his race. More French than a Frenchman, which means just too French, his ambitions are usually one of twain: either — if he is not one already — he has hopes of being a General, or else he desires to retire for the close of his life to Paris.

Personally the political gentleman is for this part of the world a well-dressed man. You meet him in all public places in a black frock-coat and straw hat. He talks with many gesticulations. He brags with a wonderful fluency. When there is no revolution going on, and there has not been a real one for eleven years, he is polite, theatrical, showy and kind-hearted. He is always shaking hands, and he is mostly a General.

One is presented. He takes off his hat and shakes hands, and you are swept up into conversation in a moment. He expects you to drink with him; indeed, he desires this ceremony so strenuously that it is well in Hayti to be a teetotaler. He is not reserved, and he dislikes your being so. He is ready to strip off the cloak of his privacy and to take you for a stroll into his personal affairs. And yet not quite inside.

There is always a well-defined line in the confidence between the white man and the black, be he of Asia or of Africa, that is seldom over-stepped. It is the reticence of race which has its source in congenital differences which are seldom bridged, and it is by reason of these that the relations between them so often fall short of mutual understanding.

The Haytian wears a goatee, but his face tells the tale of his descent. He is very touchy, and if he tries to "get at" you over any question, and you listen quietly and smile, he shrinks back at once and changes the subject. He has a horror of ridicule, and perhaps some dim apprehension of his own lack of knowledge.

He is very hospitable, and will always play to an audience. He is excessively ambitious, and will readily bow the knee to Baal. He is often brave, but fails in power of continuity of thought and effort. He cannot forego the small praise of to-day for the great success of to-morrow.

He does not talk much of his own country, unless you get him alone, but he will readily give you his opinion of every other country under the sun, and if you speak of Paris, he will blossom out into plentiful and real enthusiasm. His views on most subjects are catchy, and he never quite forgives you for being white.

From half-past twelve, when the offices close for lunch, until half-past two, when they open again, you find him everywhere. He sits in the cafes smoking a dark Havana cigarette, which does not go out, but burns away to ash if you leave it. In the cool of the day, he rides outside the town, still clad in his frock-coat, on a small horse that ambles comfortably. All round Port-au-Prince are his houses, and very nice houses they are, broad, cool, open, tropical, half-hidden in a luxuriance of trees and greenery.

Whether he believes in the future of his country I cannot say, but he is wordily and wildly attached to its independence. He can always tell you what would be its salvation, but each time he will tell you something different. In his own mind, he is often largely mixed up with its salvation himself. He is a red-hot politician, and often related to a former President. He is easy in morals, and his motto is: "Let us eat and drink, for to-morrow we die." In religious matters he is a tolerant Roman Catholic, and if you press him about the present condition of things among the masses he will shrug his shoulders and talk of Toussaint l'Ouverture.

In all ways he would model himself upon his Parisian proto-type. With his whole heart and soul he admires France ; on that one point he is absolutely sincere. Moreover, he regards the rest of the world through French eyes. This peculiarity is encouraged by his newspapers : he has two of them which retail telegrams and opinions taken from French sources and from no other. Neverthe-less, they are to the Haytian the actual mirror of all that is passing between the poles.

He is a warm partisan, and during the Spanish-American War he drank cocktails to the success of Spain, just as he drank them at the time I was in Hayti to the success of the Boer. England

and America are bugbears to Hayti. Individually, I believe, he likes the Englishman, but he cordially hates England — or, rather, that presentation of John Bull with the large and taloned hands, by the creation and perpetuation of whom the French journalists have striven to avenge all things from Waterloo to Fashoda, or, perhaps one should say to Dreyfus, for whose existence we are apparently held to be responsible.

A General, an ex-Minister of War, hoped the Boers would beat us. He was asked why. Because he had gathered from a French print that Boers were negroes persecuted by the British. He was, however, open to conviction, and, after the explanation was given, said naively that he thought all people in Africa must be black 1 In what other land could this happen?

The most blatant talkers are frequently bewildering and astonishingly ignorant. Exception must be made in favour of those who have been educated in France.

The negro is, considering his numbers, most conspicuously absent from the middle class. He forms the lower, and he predominates in the governing, but from the best class of Haytian society he is largely self-excluded. He is not, with some exceptions, at home there.

The best class of Haytian does not touch politics. He knows too well how much there is to lose and how little to gain under existing circumstances. But, then, the best class of Haytian is often a mulatto. If you were to pick out the most advanced and promising men in the Republic, you would choose a very small proportion of the pure blacks among them.

In this connection I asked a gentleman who knows as much of Hayti as any living man, if, after his long residence in the island, he really considered the negro educated up to — in fact, fitted for — the task of self-government. He replied that he believed he could put his hand on a score or two of coloured men, and a few, very few, pure-bred negroes who were certainly capable. But when I asked him why such men did not come forward for the sake of their country, he shook his head.

"They are hopelessly in the minority," he said, "and they know it."

To-day the Government is centred in a group of ultranegro proclivities, who look with an almost ferocious suspicion upon the small party who, were they to come to power, might do lasting good. But it must be remembered that the unalterable tradition of Hayti is, Hayti for the black as distinguished from the mulatto.

It has been advanced that there must be progress, since the people, or, rather, the politicians, " revolute" much less frequently than they used to do. How far this improvement in conduct is a sign of inward grace is open to question. The Haytian man of politics is not quite a fool, and he is pretty well aware that there are countries who might not put up with him if events boiled over too often especially if they boiled over with the accompaniments of bloodshed which have signalised his revolutions in the past.

The following open letter from a political Haytian is drawn entirely from views expressed in various pamphlets by Haytian writers, and is given in as close a rendering as possible of the French.

" Mon ami, — Now that evil war has ceased from the land, and peace, the beautiful, has for some years dwelt amongst us, the time has come for us, the piously devoted sons of Hayti, to be silent no longer, in face of the mistakes and deceptions that promise to ruin our country.

"We are credulous, we are well-disposed, we believe in the
false friends who run from the ends of the earth to enrich themselves at our expense. On all sides promises are lavished upon us
and miracles of prosperity are predicted should we yield to the
voice of the charmer. One would exploit the treasures of timber
in our virgin forests; some plead for concessions to begin mining

operations; others dream of railroads, canals, telegraphs, irrigation works, bridges, and lighthouses.

"They caress us, these beggars, for do we not possess to-day the wealth of Hayti?

"But behind our backs these perfidious villains, what do they not say of us? They call us a "nation of monkeys!" They say we are human crabs, who do not advance in the march of civilisation, but move always backwards. In saying this they add we must be driven forward — they propose a foreign protectorate. Before it is too late let us guard ourselves against these adventurers, these liars. Let us do nothing blindly, hastily, in the dark, at the gallop.

"Listen, while I sound the trumpet of danger!

"Let us not forget Poland, who confided herself to strangers. It was they who killed her!

"Let us recollect Egypt.

"Fifty years ago to whom did Egypt belong? To the Egyptians. A singular fury to become civilised inflamed them. Fatal disease! They were promised prosperity, they gave concessions for canals, railways, docks. Have they benefited by these things? No I All concessions have been converted into fetters for the once free limbs of Egypt, One day she awoke to find herself under the boots of England. Formerly the Egyptians were whipped and oppressed in the name of the Koran, but at least the tyrants who despoiled them were of their own blood and born in their midst, speaking the same language, professing the same religion as themselves. Are they happier to-day, when they are whipped in the name of the Bible, when British howitzers stand ready to blow into pieces those patriots who raise a voice in the defence of their liberties?

"Let us beware; let us not imitate them. Let us avoid the stranger; let us spurn his attentions! Hayti is a maiden of generous proportions. We must not allow her to give herself in marriage save to her own sons!

"Let us take precautions. Arm! Fortify! Intrench ourselves! Practise the evolutions of the military! But let us be secret in our preparations. Then we can answer the stranger who calls us a race of monkeys ('un peuple de singes') — with our guns ! The hearts of our people are ready, they do not want in courage.

"The English are brave. We conquered the English.

" The French are a great nation. We drove them into the sea.

" The victorious Napoleon himself sent his myrmidons to snatch back our new-bought liberty. We hurled them back.

"For a nation of monkeys, it was colossal!

"We will be wise. We will adopt to ourselves the doctrine of Monroe, the American — Hayti for the Haytians ! Cry aloud the watchword. Repulse in a manner the most formal, the most energetic, any interference of foreign nations in the interior affairs of our country. Our history contains the illustrious names of Toussaint L'Ouverture and of Tiresias Sam. We need not despair.

"The night is dark about us, let us wait for the moon, the moon of education and of reason that soon must rise. Let us take no step in the dark. Let us endeavour to make our military organisation still more complete. They laugh at our many Generals, those others. Have they seen us on parade.? They forget that we in Hayti are born soldiers. From being a soldier those who have training advance easily to the grade of General. They forget this when they smile.

"Hayti for the Haytians! Here alone one can show a black face without receiving upon it a buffet. It is the corner of the earth sacred to our rights. Elsewhere, in Africa, in America, the black man is governed by the white. In Hayti alone the black man governs himself, the black is the equal of the white. It is here in Hayti that we prove that fact. Here we have by right and not by tolerance. In Hayti has been gained the first foothold of the doctrine of equality of nations.

"Let us sound the trumpet!

"It has been said we are incapable of guiding ourselves, that we cannot govern, yet to whom do we as a nation owe our liberty? To our forefathers! Alone they created the Haytian nation; alone, without help of any kind, they paid in gold and blood and the sweat of their brow for the right of freedom! They bought for this small portion of the great African race the right to live in independence. We do not need foreigners to aid us. Since we were born without consulting them, let us live without doing so.

"But I must tell you, my dear friend, of the progress of events.

"On Sunday there was a review on the Champ-de-Mars. What a magnificent revelation of our national resources! Uniforms, horses, soldiers, cavalry! One dreams of it in the night. Above all things let us remind our people that we are a nation of soldiers — that our very independence is rooted in a military struggle wherein the armies of Europe were worsted.

"More than that. Hayti stands for a symbol of liberty. Not the one-sided liberty that others scream about, but the true Liberty, Equality. Fraternity. which equalises the status of the black man and the white. It may be said our republic is not so large in extent as that of France or of the United States. On that I offer no opinion, but I maintain that our very existence has a meaning altogether unique.

"But to fulfil our mission, we must rid ourselves of the whites. They trade in our coast towns, they suck the lifeblood of Hayti. What do they give to us in return? Nothing but absurd and impudent projects by which they profess to assure our national credit, to improve our commerce, to ameliorate our material condition. We need money, it is true. We can borrow, but we must refuse foreign aid in disturbing the funds. We have responsible Ministers; we have the whole machinery of the State to depend upon, who will see that all is done for the national honour, the national good.

"Up to to-day have we not built our towns alone? Without the invidious help of strangers we have conducted naval, military, and commercial operations. We have tilled our own fields, we have sown, planted, and reaped. We are a people gay, light-hearted, kind. What do we need more? We have all that produces happiness. Rut, if we would not see these days of pleasure change, we must combine to keep out the foreigners, the men of different blood, those, in a word, who are jealous of our prosperity! Those who, speaking smooth things, are preparing to rob us of all! They say we neglect the education of the masses. Well, then, let us build schools. They reproach us because we have no railways, and few roads. In answer let us point to many already surveyed. They tell us we live in fine dreams, we content ourselves with great projects. Is the fact of our independence a dream? No!

"Sons of brave fathers, awake, and be warned in time! The envious peoples threaten us on all sides; they plot against our liberties, they groan to enrich themselves at our expense! If we would live, we must be on the watch day and night. The foreigner is insidious; he creeps in upon us. We must load those now amongst us with taxes; we must push back others who would follow them. Let us maintain our traditions. Let each Haytian show himself proud and of an imperious will. We are conquerors, we are free, we do not wish to fall, to degrade ourselves, to become valets and vassals. Then beware!

" And I? — I hear you say; ' Oho, here is a sly one, he says nothing of himself As for me, I remain tranquil, I am calm. I advise, I sow the seed. Some day my country will be grateful to me. The people will say, 'What do we not owe to Monsieur le General!' Does this surprise you, my friend? Already a Minister in the Cabinet, they have now made me a General of the forces of Hayti! A General of Division. I am saluted in the streets. I have chosen a green uniform. I parade the capital on my horse.

"I have deserved it, you will say, yet is my heart full of pride. My country has recognised her deliverer. Others have also been made

Generals, but that does not affect me. They are puffed up. But I, as I have said, I remain tranquil, I am calm always. Adieu, my friend. "

Agreez, etc.,

"GENERAL MILES BOBO."

16

Hayti: The Puffball

WHAT astonishes the traveller most in Hayti is that they have everything there. Ask for what you please, the answer invariably is, " Yes, yes, we have it."

They possess everything that a civilised and progressive nation can desire. Electric light? They proudly point to plant on a hill-top outside the town. Until you have had some experience of the people and the land, you are taken aback by this galloping of events. Here is a nation hidden away in the depths of the Atlantic, which is not only abreast of the times, but ahead of many towns in England. So you say to yourself.

Constitutional Government? A Chamber of Deputies, elected by public vote, a Senate, and all the elaborate paraphernalia of the law; they are to be found here, seemingly all of them. Institutions, churches, schools, roads, railways, forts. What more can you ask for?

On paper their system is flawless. If one puts one's trust in the mirage of hearsay the Haytians have all desirable things, but on nearer approach these pleasant prospects are apt to take on another complexion.

For instance, you are standing in what was once a building, but is now a spindle-shanked ghost of its former self. A single man, nursing a broken leg, sprawls on the black earthen floor; a pile of wooden beds is heaped in the north corner ; rain has formed a pool in the middle of the room, crawling and spreading into an ever wider circle as the last shower drips from the roof. Some filthy sheets lie wound into a sticky ball on two beds, one of which is overturned. A large iron washing-tub stands in the open doorway, and a black woman sits on its edge, smoking a red earthen pipe.

Now, where are you?

It would be impossible to guess. As a matter of fact, you are in the Military Hospital of the second most important town of Hayti, a State-supported concern, in which the soldiers of the Republic are supposed to be cured of all the ills of the flesh. No need to linger; you have seen all there is to see. Besides, the place is used occasionally for smallpox cases to die in.

This is how I came there. I had met a General in the street, a fine, big negro, resplendent in uniform of gaudy green, I had heard that a soldier had met with an accident the night before. The train of thought was thus supplied. Where does this ideal country, which possesses everything, put her maimed soldiers? I was new in the land and curious. It is easy to ask a question. I asked it. My friend in gold lace waved his hand towards the building I have described — from where we stood, a blot in the distance — and said, "To the Military Hospital!" For the moment I was properly impressed. "Lucky people!" I thought to myself; " everything is arranged for you by a paternal Government." But when you get to the spot the illusion fades.

It is the same with the electric light. The plant is here, but it does not act.

It is the same with the cannon. They are cannon, but they won't go off. It is the same with their railways. They are being "hurried forward," but they never progress. It is the same with everything. Everything is arranged. Everything is drafted upon paper. It seems as if, with a people so hedged in, nothing could go wrong. They simply cannot get off the paths of progress. And yet, and yet — they have begun everything — and dropped it. Then the prisons. I have read a notable code of rules referring to them, drawn up with a view to their proper maintenance. Under this system, you say again, nothing can go wrong. On reading it you picture a model house of detention, ruled wisely by grave officials with one eye on the regulations and the other on the welfare of their prisoners.

Go to the prison. Obtain admission if you can. The grave officials of your fancy are replaced by a dozen truculent vagabonds with cocomacaque clubs. The place is the haunt of disease, blow-flies, and vermin. A pestiferous swamp, surrounded by ramshackle walls, is inhabited by the starving, naked prisoners. You will be lucky if you do not bring away with you smallpox or some kindred evil as a memento. The code of regulations is for show, the prison is for use.

But while I am on the subject of prisons, let us thresh it out. If all the realists of all the nations could be formed into one realist, and all their powers of describing the disgusting could be delegated to that one chosen individual, he might write an account of the Haytian prisons and never take the imagination of his readers within miles of the reality.

Four hundred men in two enclosed yards, stale and foul with years of use. Access is gained to the interior by a gate of iron bars. Inside, a swelter of filth, green scum, diseased bodies, nakedness, and red, raw wounds (the warders keep up the supply of these last with their clubs). That is what you will see.

It is horrible, yet it is pale to the reality. Let us leave the subject for ever. I should never have entered upon it save for the hope that when this description comes to be read in Hayti, it may stir up prison reform.

As for the Government it is nominally Republican, but under existing conditions supreme power is practically concentrated in the hands of one man, who keeps the laws or breaks them according to whim or expediency. If you come to think of it, the difficulties of governing on the Republican system are almost insuperable with high officials, many of whom can neither read nor write, and whose main idea is to fill their pockets, and eventually to succeed to the headship of the State by the rawest methods of revolution. It is therefore not to be wondered at that the regime has developed into a military despotism.

The machinery of constitutional government is complete ; there are Ministers, a Senate, and a Chamber of Deputies. But these bodies have little independent power, and are expected to carry out the wishes of the President. If they do not, the head of the State promptly suppresses all symptoms of disobedience ; otherwise there ensues a revolution. Perhaps, as matters stands, personal rule is inevitable, besides being the form most popular with the masses.

Supreme power incorporated in a strong man appeals to the imagination of the ignorant. The presidents of Hayti have been not infrequently venal, corrupt, and horribly cruel, but the man who knows how to make his will felt becomes for the time the hero of the people.

The surprising part of it is that these negroes, who bear with incredible wrongs and tyrannies from their illiterate masters, would resent the mildest sway attempted by those not of their own race and colour. The lowest of the people are as frantically opposed to annexation by a white Power as are the ruling classes, and this feeling is not so much love of their insular independence as a fear of results.

When a negro gets an idea into his head, it remains there unalterable and unmodified until the day of his death, and it happens that one of the strongest certainties in the Haytian's limited field of knowledge is that if a white Power were to become supreme in his country, he himself would be forced back into slavery.

It must of course be remembered that the Haytian — speaking of him in the bulk — has no education, no intercourse with the outer world, no means of acquiring any information outside a certain narrow cast-iron set of opinions which have been handed down to him from his fathers, and which it is to the interest of the Government to keep inviolate.

I have before described the network of generals which governs the country, so there is no need for repetition. In a sentence, Hayti is governed by about a thousand generals, and as its area is approximately 10,000 square miles, it is difficult to get very far from the founts of power.

The members of the Government live in some state. One of the highest and most powerful Ministers, however, received me most haughtily at a desk set in his bedroom.

The State offices are crowded with clerks. When I went to beg an audience of the President, the office of the Minister of Foreign Affairs, an able man, was packed with secretaries, generals, and minor officials, who appeared to have nothing to do but to smoke cigarettes.

The daily life of the President, General Tiresias Augustin Simon Sam, seems to be chiefly passed in playing draughts near the window of a room opening upon a balcony which overlooks the Champ-de-Mars. Sometimes he drives in the streets attended by a numerous suite. During the time I spent in Port-au-Prince I saw him in all four times. On the whole, I cannot think his office an enviable one.

"Uneasy lies the head that wears a crown," but I would sooner take the risk of any crown than be President of Hayti. Precedent is so cheerless, as the following list shows.

Emperor Dessalines	Assassinated.
President Petion (Southern Hayti)	Died of fever.
Emperor Christophe (Northern Hayti)	Suicide.
President Boyer	Exiled.
President Herard	Deposed after four months.

Emperor Soulouque	Fled.
President Geffrard	Fled to Jamaica
President Salnave	Shot.
President Nissage-Saget	Abdicated hurriedly.
President Domingue	Fled wounded.
President Boisrond Canal	Abdicated.
President Salomon	Abdicated and fled to Cuba.
President Legitime	Fled to New York.
President Hippolyte	Died as President!
President Sam	Present head of the Republic.

There were also some others whose day of power was so brief, that I have not thought it worth while to include them.

But there is one thing common to the whole country, of which every Haytian denies the existence. Vaudoux is the one thing which they declare they have not. They tell you there is no snake-worship (I am speaking of the higher classes) within the bounds of the Repubhc. But when you betray certain knowledge of the subject, they admit that though sacrifices and savage dances may take place in other departments, no such things are known in that one in which you at the moment find yourself.

Thus in Jacmel they told me I should find Vaudoux in Port-au-Prince and the Plain of Cul-de-Sac. In Port-au-Prince, as I was actually returning from witnessing a sacrifice within the limits of the town, I was advised to go to the Cape, where alone such rites flourished. And at the Cape they told me to take ship for Jacmel, for there I would assuredly find them. As a matter of plain fact, the traveller riding across the country in any direction is quite likely, to come suddenly in view of the ceremonies in full swing. He will see the tell-tale dances, the faces smeared in blood, perhaps even the body of the black goat, the sacred sacrifice.

Nor are they grotesque pictures only ; the element of horror darkens them all, for wherever you hear the palpitating throb of the big bullock-skin drum, and wherever the votaries of Vaudoux foregather there is always the possibility that human sacrifice has been or is to be accomplished.

Oddly enough, your most prominent feeling when first you look upon these things leads you to reflect that the boys' books are all wrong, and so is popular fancy. In both the votaries of human sacrifice parade it, as objectionable barbarians indeed, but with a savage picturesqueness of their own. Here in Hayti you have all the elements of the picturesque, forests, red fires, blood, the flash of steel, the red robes of the priest. Surely the worshippers will be in keeping with the rest of the picture. But they are not. They are neither very brave nor very fierce. They are not even barbaric ; they are merely barbarians.

It was a disappointment to me, I admit it. I do not think in the whole world you could have found a more disillusioned person than myself when first I saw a sacrifice of animals to the sacred snake. I had expected a grisly crew of fanatics, I found a medley of squalid negroes. The accepted description catches some of the salient points and brings them vividly before your eyes, but it ignores the meanness of it all while it gives rein to the picturesque. You get the rude huts where the sacrificers dwell, but you are never brought face to face with the draggle, the foulness, the sordid repulsiveness.

It is moving, it is terrible, it is savage, it is grisly, we know all that, but it is also cheap, unsavoury, eminently nasty. It is a drama of realities, not played out against a background of romance, but upon a rubbish-heap with dirty straw in the foreground. And this it is which strikes you first and leaves the lasting effect and impression. If the realist would but take a turn at describing Vaudoux sacrifice, he would let you have the smell, the staleness, the ugliness, the squint and leer of it all.

So Vaudoux flourishes and electric light fails. But you are told that the Government has for some time been taking measures to suppress the one and to set the other on a working basis. But there is no symptom that they are advancing in either direction.

Can we not christen it the puff-ball system, by which all fair seeming ends in a little explosion of dust. "Only this and nothing more."

17

Can the Negro Rule Himself?

CAN the negro rule himself? Is he congenitally capable?

That is a question which has been mooted at various times and by various writers. In nearly all cases the line of argument has been the same The negro apologist has selected some examples of great men of negro race, has used them as the foundation of his logical edifice, and instead of arguing from the masses to the individual, has reversed the order of things, and has argued from the individual to the masses.

Can the negro rule himself?

The present condition of Hayti gives the best possible answer to the question, and, considering the experiment has lasted for a century, perhaps also a conclusive one. For a century the answer has been working itself out there in flesh and blood. The negro has had his chance, a fair field and no favour. He has had the most fertile and beautiful of the Carribbees for his own; he has had the advantage of excellent French laws; he inherited a made country, with

Cap Haytien for its Paris, " Little Paris," as it was called. Here was a wide land sown with prosperity, a land of wood, water, towns, and plantations, and in the midst of it the Black Man was turned loose to work out his own salvation.

What has he made of the chances that were given to him?

To begin with, we must define the term "negro," and it is this definition that we find at the root of so many errors. The negro referred to here is the full-blooded African, not the man of mixed race, the Alexandrian, the Numidian, the Moor, or the white throw-back who has inherited a dash of the tar-brush. It is possible by arguing from the individual outwards to prove anything on earth. This fact is sufficiently obvious to need no demonstration. And yet in the whole history of the Haytian Republic there is only one instance which could give any solid support to the pro-negro line of argument —Toussaint l'Ouverture

Here we certainly find a great historical figure. Born a slave, his grandfather, it has been said, was an African prince. Judging from his pictures, you cannot but form the opinion that Toussaint was not a pure-blooded negro; the features, the shape of the head, the setting of the eyes are all so many strong reasons against such a supposition.

Among all the leaders that jostle each other in the story of Haytian Independence, his is the only name untainted by obloquy, or unsmirched by the memory of some foul and savage massacre.

In Toussaint you have a man whose word was his bond, whose acts of mercy are the sole bright episodes against one of the darkest backgrounds of history. A man really *sans peur et sans reproche*, who was actuated throughout his life by no other feeling than that of love for his country. The many tales of his acts of generosity, no one of which militated in any degree against the cause of Haytian liberty, are legion.

Over against him stands a far different figure, that of General Dessalines, who spared no man in his anger and no woman in his lust, who was corrupt and venal to an unheard-of degree. The man who crystallised his political tenets in the famous saying: "Pluck the fowl, but take care she does not cry out," a saying which to this day is honoured in the observance throughout every department of the Government. The man who ordered a woman to be beaten to death at Les Cayes under the most horrible circumstances, and around whose name each story or legend which has gathered merely adds one other instance of his cruelty.

To-day, in Hayti, which of these two men is the national hero? It is Dessalines.

And the act upon which his fame chiefly rests is the barbarous decree issued by him for the massacre of every living French soul, man, woman and child. From Toussaint, then, if he was a negro — and this I do not concede — an argument might be built up which would be, at all events to some extent, a vindication of the claim of the negro race to rule itself. But by their own choice and their own act the Haytian people have chosen Dessalines as their national hero.

There is no space here to pass in review the score or so of rulers Hayti has known. Suffice it to say that her best President was Geffrard, a mulatto, and that the dictatorship of her black Heads of State has always been marked by a redder smear than usual upon the page of history. The better, the wiser, the more enlightened and less brutalised class has always been composed of the mulattoes, and the blacks have recognised the fact, and hated the mulatto element accordingly.

But to pass from the earlier days of independence to more recent times. We had not long ago the savage rule of President Salomon, a notorious sectary of snake-worship, beneath whose iron hand the country groaned for years, and public executions, assassinations, and robbery were the order of the day. And at the present time?

To-day in Hayti we come to the real crux of the question. At the end of a hundred years of trial, how does the black man govern himself? What progress has he made? Absolutely none. When he undertakes the task of government, he does so, not with the intent of promoting the public weal, but for the sake of filling his own pocket. His motto is still, "Pluck the fowl, but take care she does not cry out."

Corruption has spread through every portion and every depart-ment of the Government. Almost all the ills of the country may be traced to their source in the tyranny, the ineptitude, and the improbity of those at the helm of state.

Port-au-Prince, the seat of Government, is the cesspool of the Republic. The reason is obvious. The capital is filled with men who are in the employ of the Government, but who are seldom paid ; indeed, who are rather expected to make use of their positions to pay themselves, and who therefore go to make up a class grasping, dishonest, discontented, and dangerous. It is not overstating the case to say that the ambitions of the average Haytian politician on entering office are not towards the advancement of his country or projects of reform ; his main idea is to make a fortune for him-self and to use his power to avenge his personal resentments. In the former connection there is a national proverb, which may be rendered: " It is no robbery to rob the State."

The bond, therefore, which consolidates a Government is not that the Ministers hold similar opinions or political convictions; it is one of common interest in keeping the ship of State under way while they help themselves as liberally as possible from its treasure-room. Suppose the present Government fell to-morrow, there is not one member of it whose first impulse would not be to put leagues of sea between himself and his native land.

Since the Black Republic arose out of the ashes of the French Revolution, it has been twice an Empire, and a Republic for the rest of the time — nominally. But under whatever category the Government may for the moment have stood, it has always been in reality a military despotism. It is that to-day, and it is possible to bribe your way to almost anything. Republicanism is, after all, a perilous form of government for a young nation, its bounds are so wide and it gives room for the working of mutual jealousies as well as infinite scope to the ambitions of the individual. "France a Republic, America a Republic, Hayti a Republic," so say the Haytians. The saying needs no comment.

I have been assured, however, by a European who has long resided in the country that there exists to-day a section of negroes who if they could win their way to power would soon make a beneficial change in the condition of things. I own that I have seen but slight trace of such a class. Besides, there seems to be little doubt that the advent into the arena of active politics of a truly patriotic party would be resented in the most lively manner by the bigoted populace, who would regard any measures of reform or progress as indicative of a design to sell them into the hand of the white, and thus back under the old yoke of slavery. This belief it is the policy of the Government to keep alive and active.

The lower classes have for their idols black generals, who can neither read nor write, whose sole claim to notoriety is their supernormal fierceness and push. And when all is said and done it is on the influence of these men that the safety and .stability of the Government depend. They possess the ear of the multitude, they are puffed up with their own importance. While they retain their present ascendency there can be no going forward for the Republic.

Their watchword is "Hayti for the Haytians," which, being interpreted, means conservatism to savagery.

To return then to the question put at the beginning of this article.

"Les Amis des Noirs", who in the days of the French Revolution gave the black man his first hint of and help towards freedom, have long since passed away themselves, but they set the thinking world a colour-problem. For a century the answer has been working itself out in flesh and blood. Can the negro rule himself? Is he congenitally capable?

The non-proven of the Scottish courts seems hardly strong enough by way of a reply. Up to date he certainly has not succeeded in giving any convincing proof of capability, has not indeed come within measurable distance of success. I think we may go a full step beyond the non-proven. We may say that, taken en masse at any rate, he has shown no signs whatever which could fairly entitle him to the benefit of the doubt that has for so long hung about the question.

He has had his opportunity. That opportunity has lasted for a hundred years in a splendid land which he found ready prepared for him. Yet to-day we find him with a Government which, save in the single point of *force majeure,* has degenerated into a farce; and as for the country itself, houses and plantations have disappeared, and where clearings once were there is now impenetrable forest. Certainly he has existed through one hundred years of internecine strife, but he has never for six consecutive months governed himself in any accepted sense of the word. Today, and as matters stand, he certainly cannot rule himself.

FINIS